NEVER SAY NEVER

ONE WOMAN'S JOURNEY TO SURVIVE

By Celeste Roth

Copyright © 2014 by Celeste Roth
First Edition – February 2014

ISBN
978-1-4602-3453-2 (Hardcover)
978-1-4602-3454-9 (Paperback)
978-1-4602-3455-6 (eBook)

All rights reserved.

No part of this publication may be reproduced in any form, or by any means, electronic or mechanical, including photocopying, recording, or any information browsing, storage, or retrieval system, without permission in writing from the publisher.

Produced by:

FriesenPress
Suite 300 – 852 Fort Street
Victoria, BC, Canada V8W 1H8

www.friesenpress.com

Distributed to the trade by The Ingram Book Company

In *Never Say Never*, Celeste Roth writes with great skill about her difficult childhood in an abusive foster home and her subsequent challenges in both her professional and personal lives. Despite great struggles, Celeste overcomes her past and forges strong relationships with her son, her husband and her closest friends, always remembering to give them the love she missed as a child. She also scales impressive professional heights, ensuring the financial security of her loved ones.

Written in lucid, flowing prose, *Never Say Never* keeps the reader engaged throughout. This novel moves at an agreeable pace and always has its audience in mind. Congratulations to the author!

NEVER SAY NEVER

For my son, Keith . . . I'll love you forever.

And to my husband, Stephen, who's been my rock and my soft place. His wonderful heart never ceases to amaze and inspire me.

ACKNOWLEDGEMENTS

I would like to acknowledge Pam Hirson for the countless hours she's dedicated to this project, never once compromising her beliefs or values. She has my sincere gratitude for sharing her experience, ideas, and inspiration. Her professional approach has taken this book beyond anything I could have imagined, and I will always be indebted to her for making my dream come true.

NEVER SAY NEVER

*"Childhood is what you spend the rest of your
life trying to overcome.
That's what Momma always says.
She says that beginnings are scary, endings are usually sad,
but it's the middle that counts the most.
Try to remember that when you find yourself at a new beginning.
Just give hope a chance to float up. And it will..."*

Birdee Pruitt, Hope Floats –1998

CHAPTER ONE

If it's true that childhood is what you spend the rest of your life trying to overcome, then I was doing well and progressing nicely through each new beginning. So many times, when there hardly seemed to be a chance, hope had floated up again. I'm still amazed that every time I look in the mirror there's a competent woman staring back at me, instead of what might have been.

Some could argue that childhood does not define us. I'm not so sure. Whether we grow up repeating or contradicting what we've learned, our decisions are still based on the earliest and least educated years of our lives; a limited frame of reference at best.

Along the way we muddle through, stopping now and then to ask why, blaming others, and finding ways to cope. Sometimes we change and sometimes we don't, but in the end, if we're fortunate, we learn to accept who we are and why, and then we make peace with that.

Though my birth was uneventful, my life was not. While most newborns are bonding with proud parents, I was born to a mother too ill to care for a baby and a father who had no time for one. As a result, I became a ward of the state and was moved from one foster home to another, gaining momentum in neglectful care.

"On behalf of the state, I'd like to thank you for your kindness in taking another foster child, especially on such short notice, "Mrs. McDonald, my case worker said. "The poor thing's only five and as you can see, a little under-nourished. She's had it rough, but I can assure you that with a little time and patience, Celeste will do well here."

CELESTE ROTH

I'll never forget that steely eyed stare, or that intimidating frown. Her jowls, partly to blame, tugged at the corners of her mouth leaving gravity no choice. Still, a sour look was a practical companion for such deep set wrinkles and haggard appearance. To make matters worse, she chewed gum like a cow, and dressed in black... always black. With storm trooper boots, no less! Even at five I knew they didn't go with a dress.

"I'll stop in from time-to-time and check on things," Mrs. McDonald assured the Duvall's. "To make sure she's coming along." Her hand was like a clamp on my arm. I wondered where she thought I was going that she had to hold on so tight. The bulldog death grip, I remember it well. The closer she came, the stronger the stench of moth balls.

With her jaw set firm, she wagged a stubby finger at me and told me to be a good girl. Then, picked up that enormous file case of hers and walked out the door. If there was a store called "Ugly," that had to be where she shopped.

Mr. and Mrs. Duvall had wasted no time in setting ground rules. In front of a well worn sofa, I stood at attention and received the list. "Understand?" Not sure if it'd been posed as a question, I played it safe. With my arms by my sides and my lips squeezed shut, I nodded in agreement.

We'd just about finished when their eighteen-year-old daughter, Theresa, came barreling through the room, barely stopping to grunt hello. Six-year-old, Tom, was close behind her. Tom was a foster child who'd been with the Duvall's for about a year. From the look of him, he wasn't too happy about it. Then again, Theresa didn't look all that pleased, either. Still, I wasn't worried. After where I'd been, this place couldn't be much worse. Besides, there was always the hope it would be better.

It didn't take long to realize the Duvall's weren't big on patience. By the time I was seven I'd been in more trouble than any one child ought to be. Seemed I was a sorry excuse for a little girl, or at least that's what they told me. And I believed them. After all, what did

NEVER SAY NEVER

I know?

Tom turned out to be my most trusted, and only friend. He was everything I'd imagined a brother would be. Tom consoled me, watched out for me, and shared whatever he had, including his room. Life had become almost bearable because of him.

Seven was a hopeful year, but came to a disappointing close when Dad brought a Christmas tree home for us to decorate. Tom and I had been so excited that we sat on the tattered Linoleum and stared at the box of decorations for more than an hour. But our faces fell the moment we saw the sorry excuse for a tree. It was nothing but one big twig! A left over from last year; it had to be. "How are we going to decorate that?" I asked my father. Immediately, the tree fell to the ground, and *whack*; an open hand across the face. My fingers quickly covered the spot in an attempt to cool the sting.

"You wanted it; now decorate it!" Dad yelled before he stormed out of the room.

We might as well have thrown the Christmas balls on the floor, that's where most of the pine needles were anyway. Finding branches strong enough to hold the decorations took hours, but finally the lights were up and the balls glistened from wherever we could get them to stay. Everything was going fine until Mom noticed we had practically blanketed the tree with garland.

"Take some of that stuff off. There's too much on the tree." Without giving us any time to react, she'd crossed the room and grabbed the rest right out of our hands. "You can't do anything right," she scolded. I could feel my nostrils flare and fought really hard to keep my mouth shut, but the words just leaked out. "You do it!"

Smack! I didn't even see it coming that time.

"That's for answering back," Dad said. I ran outside and stayed there until the coast was clear. Then, without a sound, tiptoed back inside and managed to stay quiet and out of trouble for the rest of the day.

When Dad said it was time for bed we went without a single

complaint, hopeful that Santa would bring us gifts while we slept.

There were many nights Tom and I had stayed up late whispering in the darkness, but that night we were so excited that we babbled away almost the whole night. We'd hardly gotten any sleep at all; before we knew it the sun was shinning through the window.

"Tom, it's Christmas!" I couldn't get out of bed fast enough. All the gifts were there, tucked around the tree in neat little stacks. What if the gifts weren't for us? My stomach rolled as the thought occurred to me.

Tom didn't seem very excited, so I did my best to get him into the spirit. "Look at all those presents!"

Tom just shrugged. "Big deal, you know most of them are for Theresa and her boyfriend, Freddy. We're not their real kids. Maybe we'll get one or two, like last year. Don't go getting your hopes up for more than that. We're lucky to be getting anything at all."

My heart sank right to the bottom of my shoes and I fought to hold back the tears. They had to have more than one or two for us; with all those packages, there had to be more than that. Please make a lot of them for us. Please, please, please. Lots of toys, I pleaded silently to a God I didn't know existed.

Invisible, Tom and I sat across the room waiting while Mom and Dad opened gifts with Theresa and Freddie. There were so many presents; Tom just had to be wrong. We waited patiently, and then when everyone was finished and the floor was covered with wrappings, ribbons, and bows that would never stick again, Mom held out a gift to me. Then, she gave one to Tom. I tore into mine, anxious to find a baseball glove, bat, or even a board game. My mouth dropped when I saw the sweater. At least it wasn't a frilly looking girl sweater, but still, what kind of Christmas present was that for a kid? Tom held up his new pajamas. That wasn't any better than what I got. But I realized there was still hope when we each received a second present. Tape recorders! Finally, we'd gotten something to play with. A brand new toy and it was all mine. I couldn't have been happier, or so I thought. Then, Mom held out a third present for each of us. My

NEVER SAY NEVER

little feet jumped up and down in celebration of the most magical moment I'd ever experienced. Three presents! I'd never ever gotten three. The excitement quickly faded as I examined the doll that had been hidden inside the package. What was I going to do with a doll? Thank heaven for youthful resilience; hardly a moment had passed before I returned to my former state of euphoria. I got to unwrap three presents!

Later that day was the party at the gas station. Every year the owner held a Christmas party for the "less than fortunate" children. That was us, Tom and I, less than fortunate. We looked forward to the celebration where there'd be presents, soda, candy, and popcorn, too; lots of sugary treats that we never got to have anywhere else.

After the party was the annual family dinner. Aunts, uncles, and cousins gathered around a huge holiday table set with Christmas plates on a bright red tablecloth with matching red napkins. As usual, everyone except for the cousins ignored me, but I didn't care. I was glad there were kids to play with. Still, since nothing in my life had ever lasted very long, it didn't pay to get too excited, or too attached.

CHAPTER TWO

No matter how hard I tried to behave, I was always getting hit for something. Why was it so hard for them to love me? Maybe what they said was true, I was just unlovable.

The next seven years moved painfully slow or just painfully. Either way, every so often I'd bravely approach my mom with a question she'd prefer I hadn't asked. One I'd hoped would give me a morsel of something to hang onto, just a word or two.

At those particular moments, the need was greater than the fear and so I asked. "Mom, would you be sad if my real dad came to get me? Would you want me to stay?" My heart raced with anticipation, clinging to the tiniest shred of hope.

"You'd just have to go with him. That's all. Your father's your father. If he comes, you go." Not even close. Why couldn't she understand what I was searching for? Fighting back the lump now forming in my throat, I gave her one more chance.

"But would it bother you? Just tell me that. Would it?"

"I don't have any say in the matter," she maintained. Then, with the simple wave of a hand, she dismissed both the subject and me.

Tears streamed down my cheeks as I ran to my room, disappointed, humiliated, and angrier than ever before. If only she could have told me she loved me, or we'd work something out, but she never did and I hated her with such fierceness that it threatened my undoing.

All I ever wanted was a family who could love me—a normal life. All I wanted was to be a regular kid, anyone but me.

I got up and stood in front of the beat up old dresser and stared into the mirror that was attached at the top. Even the mirror belonged where it was. It was part of something. Speaking to my own reflection I asked, "What's wrong with me?"

Abandoning the moment, I searched for a clean sweatshirt. Sal was on his way and I didn't need any more trouble. As my biological father, Sal was entitled to visitation. Why he even wanted to visit was something I've never understood, but today was supposed to be his day.

"Why can't he just leave me alone?" I'd said it a bit too loud, and then hoped Mom hadn't heard.

She'd heard all right, and responded quickly, too. "He's your father. Don't ever forget that! Now get ready," using a tone that said you'd better not argue, or else.

Seconds later, Mom was in my room. "What's taking so long?" One look at my tear-stained eyes and red nose told her all she needed to know. "If you don't get ready right now I'll give you something to cry about. Sal's due any minute and I'm not going to be the one to sit there and entertain him. I've got better things to do with my time."

When she stormed out, I flew across the room, locking the door before she could come back. "Just leave me alone. I hate all of you! You're horrible people; horrible, horrible, horrible." My body slid down the back of the door and I sat there like a human doorstop.

My mother's response couldn't have been more threatening if she'd been holding a kettle of scalding water. "That's pretty bold talk there. Let's see what you have to say when your father comes home. You won't have such a smart mouth then." It didn't take much to figure out there was a beating headed my way.

Sal was just going to have to get along without me today. I grabbed a jacket and slipped quickly and quietly out of the window. There was no way I was coming back, not ever.

I walked and walked, then sat; walked some more, and then sat again. I'd covered a lot of ground, but didn't really seem to be getting anywhere, as if I'd had a clue where I was going anyway, but it was already late in the afternoon and my stomach started to

NEVER SAY NEVER

grumble. Empty pockets and hunger pains were not an ideal combination. Although I hadn't been there more than a handful of times, I remembered my aunt lived pretty close by. Not only was she a great cook, she was also nice. Her voice was pretty, low and sweet like the purr of a cuddly kitten.

It wasn't long before I was in front of the house summoning the courage to ring the bell, except, I wasn't quite brave enough. Instead, I turned and ran back down the steps before anyone saw me.

Hunger had almost gotten the best of me, but once I was safely around the corner there was time to think. And what I realized was the very real possibility she would call my mother. Still, the louder my stomach growled the more willing I was to risk it.

Aunt Dora stood in the vestibule, her mouth wide in surprise. "Celeste, what are you doing here? Is anyone with you, Honey? You didn't come by yourself, did you?" Looking past and around me, she'd rattled off questions one after the other. Her eyebrows lifted, and then dropped as she put an arm across my shoulders and led me inside. We sat on the oversized floral sofa, between a half-dozen fringed pillows. I could hear Aunt Dora let out a huge sigh before she smiled. In a sweet voice she asked how I'd managed to turn up at her door. "Does your mother know you're here?"

My feet dangled above the shiny wood floor, twisting and turning, the backs of my sneakers banging into the couch. Fear washed over me like a flood. I took a deep breath and swallowed. "I walked. And no, I don't think she does, exactly. But she knows I'm okay. I'm sure of that." My stomach let out a lion sized growl.

"Heavens! Looks like we've got more important things to take care of right now," she'd said with a brilliant smile. "How about if I fix you something to eat? Maybe a sandwich? I think there's some turkey in the refrigerator."

"Great! Yes, I mean thank you." I stood fast, my eagerness clearly visible.

Aunt Dora made a place for me at the table, setting out a pretty placemat that had a ruffle all the way around it. "Here you go,

Celeste. Start on these while I fix that sandwich for you." She put a glass of milk and a small plate of home-made chocolate chip cookies on the table. "Help yourself."

"Mmm, these are good," I said, in-between some very unlady-like bites.

"Save room for your sandwich; it'll be ready in a minute."

All I could manage was a semi-smile while I stuffed cookie after cookie into my mouth.

Aunt Dora put another plate in front of me; this time it was a turkey sandwich cut into four pieces, and she'd gone to the trouble of cutting the crust off the bread. I really wished I could live with her. "Your mother's probably worried sick. I think I'll go and give her a call while you're eating, just to let her know you're safe."

"No, no, no." I held up the one minute finger as I tried to swallow my food. "That's not necessary; I'll go home right after I finish this."

"Celeste, would you like to tell me what's going on? Is everything all right at home?"

"Everything's fine. Really. It is."

Her face twisted with doubt. Clearly she could see there were holes in my story. She left the room in spite of my protest. I knew time was about to run out and trouble was on its way, so half-standing, I chomped down what was left of my sandwich, grabbed a couple of cookies, and bolted right out of the back door. It would have been a good plan except my uncle happened to be walking in the back door at that exact moment. Boom! I crashed right into him.

"Whoa there, slow down. Celeste, where are you off to in such a hurry?"

I twisted and turned, and tried to wriggle myself from his grip, but he wasn't about to let me go. When Aunt Dora came back into the kitchen, she took one look at the scene by the kitchen door and ordered everyone to sit. "What is going on, Celeste? Please tell us why you're so afraid that you had to try and sneak out of here while I called your folks. We only want to help you, but we can't do anything unless you tell us what's wrong." That was the one thing I couldn't do. The beating would've been worse if I told. Jack'd probably murder me, or worse.

When the door bell rang terror tore through me. My body shook and I cried in fear that they were going to kill me this time. I waited for the damning words that never came. It was eerily silent; there wasn't a peep the whole way home, not from me, or them.

When we walked into the house, Sal was still there.

"What's your problem?" He said with disgust. "Why do you have to be so ungrateful? These people are trying to care for you and all you do is give them trouble. I wouldn't blame them if they kicked your sorry butt out of here."

With my head bowed in disgrace, I stood silently as he lashed out at me again and again. "We don't know what to do with you," the Duvall's added. "One more stunt like that and you're going to the State Home. That's where they put the misfits: runaways, dummies, and little thieves." I didn't even look up, just fought back the tears. "Your nothing but trouble everywhere you go." Battle lost. With tears streaming I was sent to my room in disgrace, banished from their sight.

With my ear pressed to the closed door I listened to the three of them strategizing, unsuccessfully.

"It's late. Let's sleep on it and discuss this in the morning." My mother had suddenly become the voice of reason.

Once Sal left the beating was sure come. With that in mind I ran up to him pleading, "Take me with you, please. They'll beat me if you don't."

He grabbed me by the arm and squeezed it tight. "You'll stay right here until they decide what to do with you. How am I supposed to take care of you if I have to work? Now, I'm going home and you had better behave yourself." His voice was stern, his face twisted with meanness.

"Can I have something to drink?" I asked as my eyes searched the floor.

"Guess you're not as smart as you thought, running away.

Kitchen's closed. Now go to bed!" Dad ordered and I went without protest, relieved to have gotten off as easy as I did.

Tossing and turning, it occurred to me I wasn't going to fall asleep until I had a drink. My mouth was cottony dry. As soon as I heard the snoring from my parent's room, I tiptoed quietly down the hall, past their door, and into the kitchen.

"What are you doing?" Stunned, I turned around to find my mother standing by the counter. How she could've gotten in here without me hearing her.

"I'm thirsty." There was no need to lie.

"Fine. Get something to drink and get back to bed before your father hears you."

She didn't yell, or wake Jack, just went back to bed.

The next morning, not a word was said about the day before. It was strange, like an alternate universe where everything looked the same, but nothing was as it should be. It was unsettling.

After school, the mystery of the morning had been solved. I came home to find Bulldog McDonald parked on the sofa. That steely eyed stare of hers was ready to burn a whole right through my head. She didn't waste a minute. "Why did you run away?" It sounded more like an accusation than a question and I wondered if she really expected me to answer, risking life and limb?

My mother's voice broke the unnatural silence. "We don't know what her problem is. We've tried everything, but we just don't know what to do with her anymore."

"If she continues this behavior we'll have to place her in reform school," the bulldog snarled.

CHAPTER THREE

Four times a year I was taken to the Foundling Hospital for a physical, whether I needed one or not. It was the responsibility of the state to make sure I was healthy, so Mom would drag me over there to have my file updated, proof that everyone had done what they were supposed to do.

The worst part, naturally, was when they gave me a shot or took blood. I hated getting stuck with those awful needles. "Don't be a baby," the nurse would insist, every time she'd jam one into my arm. I wondered what was wrong with everyone. Was there some kind of sign above my head that said it was okay to mistreat me? I just didn't get it.

As time went on I developed agonizing headaches, and along with them came numbness on my left side. There didn't seem to be any answers as to why I had them, but the medication the doctor's had prescribed didn't help at all. It would take days to shake the symptoms and no matter what tests were run, they came back inconclusive. For lack of a better answer, the doctors suggested that emotional problems could be the underlying cause of my symptoms. I was referred to a psychiatrist for further evaluation.

The following week, Mrs. McDonald took me to see Doctor Stein.

"Hello, there. What's your name?"

"Celeste," I replied with caution.

"What a beautiful name! Just like you, sweetheart." A huge smile crossed my face. No one had ever spoken to me like that. I wondered if it was a trick. I'd have to be careful until I was sure of what he was up to. He introduced himself as Dr. Stein. "Come, let's talk in my office." He pointed to a door on the other side of the waiting room, and then waited for me to take the first step. His office was large. There was a desk with two chairs in front of it and one chair behind it. Dr. Stein sat behind his desk and I sat in one of the two chairs in front.

"Can I ask you some questions, Celeste? I'd like to get to know you a little better." After I nodded in agreement, he asked where I lived, if I liked it there, and if I missed my biological father. Those questions seemed okay, but I still needed to be careful. There was no doubt that whatever I said would end up in my file and if it was something that got back to the Duvall's I'd get a beating for sure.

Very carefully, I tried to answer. "I don't really know my father too well, so I guess I can't miss what I never had, and I'm not too crazy about my life in general, but I guess it isn't anyone's fault."

He gave a sort of chuckle at my diplomatic and well thought out answer. Then, he asked if I knew what would make me happy.

"Well, I'd like it if I had real parents and a home that no one could take me away from. That would help."

"In time, Celeste, I'm sure you'll have that." He smiled, and then he asked if there was anything that was bothering me.

"No, I don't think so."

"Well, tell me about the Duvall's. Are they nice people?"

"They're okay, I guess." My eyes stayed fixed on my shoes for fear he'd see I was lying.

"Do they ever hit you?" I wanted to be honest, but I didn't want to risk a beating.

"Sometimes, but not very often, and it's only when I'm bad."

"Are you often bad?"

"Well, it does look that way, but I just think people don't like me very much."

"How could anyone not like a pretty girl like you?"

I grinned. Pretty. He thought I was pretty.

"What about games, do you like to play games?"

"Games? What kind of games?" That's when he brought out

Monopoly and we played for a while.

We had a great time that day and each session after that. Those weekly visits were the highlight of my life because Dr. Stein was the one person who was nice to me. I wanted to live with him and his family. I even asked if I could be his foster child. "The state will pay you," I tried enticing him.

"Celeste," he smiled as he said my name. "Although it sounds like a very nice idea, I'm sure your family would miss you."

"Oh, they won't care. You're the only one who does care about me."

"That's not true, Celeste, and someday you'll come to understand that."

When his evaluation was complete our visits came to an end. He called in the old bulldog to join us, and explained that he found nothing wrong with me. I remember how he said it. "She just needs a little reassurance that her family loves her."

To me, he said, "You're a good girl, Celeste. I've enjoyed our talks. Take care of yourself and remember to do the best you can within your circumstances."

On our way out, Dr. Stein's secretary, Marcy, gave me a squeeze and said, "Stop by and visit us anytime you're in the neighborhood." They were the nicest people I'd ever met. I hoped there were more like them.

The minute we got home I ran straight to the backyard to play until my father came home. When he pulled into the driveway, I was all excited to show him the model airplane the doctor had helped me to build. "Do you want to see it? He gave it to me to take home."

"Not now. Get in the house and help your mother with dinner."

After dinner, I showed him my model. "This is what the state does with taxpayer's money? What a joke!"

Disappointed, I went to my room, planted myself face down on the bed, and cried. Afterward, I prayed for a family that would love me just the way I was, and then drifted off to sleep, hoping by morning it would happen.

CHAPTER FOUR

While I was at school, the guidance counselor had called my mother to discuss my late arrivals. Mom had whacked me good when I got home. When Dad came home he let me have it too, right in the face. I expected that, but I never saw the second one coming.

"I hate you and I wish you were dead!" I screamed between sobs and ran out of the house. This time I stayed on the steps in front. Running away last time hadn't worked out too well. I wasn't going to make that mistake again. A very long fifteen minutes later, I was told to go inside and get to bed.

The next morning, the bulldog was back.

"She's a problem, and we just don't know what to do with her." It seemed I was always in trouble for something and they didn't know how much more they could take. As tears trickled, Mrs. McDonald grabbed my arm and shook me hard.

"You'd better pay attention in school and get there on time. Do you hear me? You need to appreciate what you have." She pointed her finger at my face and threatened, "One more problem and you're going to reform school. Is that what you want?" I'd lost control and sobbed so hard I couldn't catch my breath. I didn't care anymore. I just wanted my life to be over.

Everything seemed to quiet down as I sat on my bed trying to collect myself. Little did I know they were getting ready for the next round.

When they called me back into the kitchen, Mrs. McDonald put one of her chubby hands on my arm while the other one cupped my chin.

She gave me that steely eyed stare and asked, "Do you understand what we've told you?"

There was no point in saying anything; I don't think they expected an answer anyway.

"If you don't do what you're supposed to, young lady, it'll be impossible to place you anywhere. I'll have to put you in a home for bad girls."

"I'm not bad," I shouted in my own defense. "I'm good! You're just a bunch of old, nasty people. I hope you all die."

I ran back to my room and locked the door, and then slid the night stand over, jamming it against the back of the door. I hoped barricading myself in would keep me safe. "You open that door and come out here, this instant. We're not finished with you," the bulldog bellowed as she banged on the hollow door.

Shaking, I crawled out the window and ran around the corner to a friend's house. When I explained to her mother what was happening, she let me stay for a while, just long enough to calm down before she walked me home.

"Thank you, Mrs. Shay, for bringing Celeste home. We're sorry she bothered you."

The door closed softly, but as soon as she was out of earshot, *whack!*

"That's for telling people what's going on in our house. What goes on here stays here." *Whack!* "And God help you if you ever open your mouth again," Jack warned.

The next day, I had trouble concentrating at school, so it was no surprise when the teacher called on me and I didn't have the answer. Mrs. Kramer was the tallest of all the teachers, six feet tall and rail thin. Every hair was perfectly ordered and her outfits were always beautifully coordinated. Mrs. Kramer was known as the strictest teacher in the school, but everyone liked her. Thankfully, she took pity on me that day because I wasn't up for another beating quite so soon.

Mrs. Kramer was in charge of the Glee Club. Every Christmas, the club would walk up and down the hall singing Christmas carols. I wanted desperately to be a part of that group, but you had to be a straight A student and you couldn't get into any trouble, none at all. That let me out, on both counts. Still, I desperately wanted to be one of them. With nothing to lose, I summoned the courage to ask Mrs. Kramer if I could join.

"Can you sing?"

"Yes! And I'm really good, too." She let me audition, and then signed me up on the spot. There was, however, one condition; I'd be out at the first sign of trouble. The excitement was overwhelming and I jumped up and down, thanking her repeatedly.

"Now get back to class before I change my mind," she warned, but grinned at the same time.

I couldn't wait to get home and share the good news. I ran the whole way.

"That's nice, but if you don't behave we'll pull you right out. Got it?" That was my mother's less than enthusiastic reply.

"I'll be good; I promise! You'll see." This was the best thing ever. Finally, something I could be a part of. "Everyone will look at us when we walk down the hall at Christmas," I continued sharing the details with my mother until my father walked in. "Dad!" He'd just cleared the door when I bounced into the living room and stood practically on top of him, excited to share my news. "I sang great today. I'm in the Glee Club! You should have heard me . . . "

"Glee Club? How'd you manage that when you're so bad in school?" Boom. He got me again and didn't even use his hands that time.

I cried into my pillow that night, hoping no one would hear me. Tom heard, but didn't say a word. He just pretended to be asleep. That's what we'd both learned to do, give each other a little privacy to get over the sting.

The next day I did my best to be good, not make jokes, laugh out loud, or answer teachers back. Things were going well and I even raised my hand to answer questions. But for some reason the teacher was calling on all the other kids and not me. She was probably tired of me giving the wrong answers, which I usually did, but when I had to go to the bathroom and Mrs. Kramer still ignored me, I kept my hand up, even as she moved on to the next lesson.

"Mrs. Kramer, Mrs. Kramer," I called out, as my hand waved wildly in the air. "I need to be excused to go to the bathroom." Still, she ignored me. Finally, becoming more and more urgent, I stood up and asked if I could leave the room. "Please," I said.

"Sit down, Celeste, right now."

"But . . .Please, Mrs. Kramer. I can't wait any longer. I really have to go."

"Wait for recess."

"Mrs. Kramer . . ." I continued to plead.

"If you leave you'll be sent to the principal's office, so I suggest you sit back down." And that's just what I did because I didn't want her any more upset than she already was for fear of being thrown out of the Glee Club. But I was never as embarrassed as that moment when I piddled right there in my seat. My dress was soaked. The kids were hysterical. Mrs. Kramer walked over to me, grabbed me by the hand, and sent me to the office.

My mother came right away with dry clothes. She was upset with my teacher and confronted her. "Why didn't you let her go to the bathroom?"

"She's generally causing trouble and I was in no mood, so I ignored her. I'm terribly sorry."

The incident was reported to the principal, and I was returned to class. By that time, I'd developed one of those awful migraines with spots, blurred vision, and numbing on my left side. Mrs. Kramer took me to the nurse who called my mother to come and get me.

"She's more trouble than she's worth," I heard my father say that night, as my mother recounted the details of the day.

Two days later, the headache had finally gone away and I was able to go back to school.

"Baby, baby," the kids called out when they saw me. "You should wear diapers," they taunted.

Humiliated, I screamed back, "Leave me alone." Then, pushed them aside and ran off to hide. Naturally, the teacher reported me for fighting with the other children.

"It wasn't my fault," I tried to explain, but the principle was adamant.

"It's time to teach you a lesson you won't forget." She took me by the hand, walked me straight into the kindergarten room and put me in the time-out corner, ordering me to stand there until the end of the session. The little kindergarteners thought it was hysterical. The last of my dignity was now gone. Mortified, I bolted from the classroom and flew down the steps, tears spilling onto my cheeks. At one point, I lost my footing and bumped into a teacher who was walking up. It was an accident and completely unintended when I knocked her to one side.

By the time the principle caught up with me, the story was that I had intentionally and without cause pushed the teacher down the stairs. Once again, no one wanted to listen and I was suspended for two days. I was also kicked out of the Glee Club.

"Please," I pleaded with Mom not to tell Jack.

"You'll just have to face the consequences," she said.

"But it's all a giant mistake. I didn't do anything. Really, I didn't. Why can't you believe me?"

When Jack came home from work I hid under the bed. Mom filled him in on the details and it didn't take long before his booming voice was calling out for me. "Celeste, get your sorry little butt in here, now." Too terrified to move a muscle, I stayed put, frozen to the spot. It couldn't have been more than a few seconds when he stormed in and ordered me out from under the bed. He reached under, grabbed my arm and pulled me out. That was the worst belt lashing I'd ever gotten. When he finally dropped his belt to the floor I backed away inching closer and closer to the door, but there was still fire in his eyes. He caught my arm before I could run, and then used his other hand to wallop me in the face.

Mom tried to pull him off. "Jack, stop it, you'll kill her," she screamed in terror. "Please, Jack, stop!" she pleaded.

The screaming stopped as suddenly as his fists did. Like a tormented animal, I was writhing in pain. There were awful sounds coming out of me. I brought my hands to my face trying to soothe the throbbing, but when I looked down at them they were bathed in blood.

"Look at her," my mother screamed. "How are you going to explain that, Jack?"

"Get rid of her. I've had enough of these foster kids. She'd better be gone when I get home tomorrow, or I swear I'll kill her. And then I'll kill you." Jack stormed out of the house after that.

Neither Mom nor I moved an inch until the front door slammed shut. She helped me into the bathroom and cleaned the blood from my face. Tired and weak, I just collapsed to the floor. That's where I stayed, and slept until morning.

I didn't look much better in the morning, and since it was Friday my mother kept me home from school. She'd hoped that by Monday I'd be healed enough that no one would suspect anything.

Thank goodness Tom had been away for a few days or Jack would have been dead by now, and Tom would have been in jail. As the years passed, Tom had grown pretty big, big enough that when he warned Jack about touching him, Jack listened. Hopefully, by the time Tom came back, I'd be healed enough to downplay the whole thing. I couldn't live with myself if Tom got into trouble over me.

That left Sal. Mom called to postpone his Saturday visit. She said I was sick and that she didn't want him to catch anything. Sal showed up anyway, in spite of my mother's phone call, so she told him I got hurt playing outside. She explained that I hadn't listened when she warned me to stop climbing the big oak out back. And that's exactly what happened, I fell out of the tree, scraping my face on some branches. My injuries, they agreed, had been the result of my disobedience.

CHAPTER FIVE

No matter how I'd hoped or prayed, nothing changed. I hated my life. I hated everyone who was ever mean to me, especially the kids who laughed at me. Mom would let Theresa cut my hair and she was no haircutter. She'd also dress me in hand-me-down clothing, which was always a size too big or small. The kids called me ugly, teasing me mercilessly, laughing at the sight of me.

Dad's answer any time I dared to complain was, "If you don't like it around here, pack your bags."

Around the house I had chores. And they had to be done before I could go out and play. It wasn't as if I had anyone to play with, but I'd watch the other kids play.

Tom never understood why I even bothered. "Don't go near them," he'd tell me. It was sound advice, but what else was there to do? I secretly hoped that one day they'd let me play. Tom would go after them every so often and threaten them, defending my honor when they teased me.

Now and then, a neighbor would take pity on me and invite me over to play, but that didn't happen often. Tom and I were the foster kid outcasts, different from everyone else.

Theresa wasn't as bad as all the others. There were times when she'd take me out for the afternoon, if she had nothing better to do. We were both mesmerized by planes taking off and landing, so we'd head over to the airport and watch them. It wasn't very often, but it was nice.

No matter how everyone else treated us, Mom and Dad were the worst. Tom and I would pretend not to hear when Dad would yell at Mom, "Get rid of those little brats! I don't want them around anymore." They'd argue and fight, Dad's anger escalating until he eventually hit her, always in the face or throat.

Tom and I felt so bad that no one wanted us that we packed a bag and planned to run away. Dad came in the room and caught us. We both got a beating that night.

It was impossible to stay out of trouble. We were always getting blamed for something or other. When Tom had gotten too big and was better able to defend himself, Jack called his social worker to come and get him. I begged and pleaded, "Don't take him; he's all I have. Please!" She took him anyway.

Then there was just me. "Why do you hate me so much?" I asked my Dad. "Is it possible that you could find a way to love me, even just a tiny bit?"

"I don't hate you, Celeste. I just don't want to deal with any of this anymore. I don't need those social workers coming around, looking into my business, and telling me how to live my life. That's all it is."

That's how I lived, in fear of being moved to a different foster home, just like Tom. And what would happen to me there? It was a risk I didn't want to take. I tossed and turned through the night, pretending I was someone else, anyone else but me.

CHAPTER SIX

All I wanted was to be treated as if I mattered. Mike was a neighbor who used to talk to me once in a while. One day he offered to take me out for a soda. I hesitated at first, but I knew I would enjoy the attention as well as the soda. And I was right. It turned out to be a lot of fun. We laughed and talked; it felt great to have someone who wanted to spend time with me.

The following week he asked if I'd like to go for a ride in his brand new sports car. It was a convertible, fire engine red. I'd never been in a new car before, or in any car that came close to that one.

"Sure!" We drove all over Queens, and then he treated me to lunch. It was one of the few really nice days I'd had. After that, Mike would invite me to take rides whenever he saw me. Sometimes, he'd take me shopping and buy me little trinkets. No one had ever done that before. I never told anyone about it, or showed them anything he'd bought for me. Mike was older, in his twenties, and I didn't want anyone to get the wrong idea about him. He was just being nice to me and I appreciated it. He made me feel special and we became good friends.

One day, he asked me to come over to his house. That I couldn't do. I explained that my parents would never allow it.

"We don't have to tell them," he said.

I knew it would be wrong to go and if my folks found out, I'd be in a heap of trouble. But it was nice having a friend to do things with and I really did want to see his house . . .

"Okay, let's go," I said.

At first, we watched a little TV, told a few jokes, and then he took me out to a nice restaurant. It was the first time I'd been inside a place like that, with tablecloths and china dishes. The following week, he invited me over again. He'd said he got a movie for us to watch. I smiled. He was always doing nice things like that. It was new to me, but I did enjoy having someone who wanted to spend time with me.

We sat on the couch as the movie started. He told me I would like this one; it was a little different, but I should give it a chance. From the shocked look on my face it was easy to tell that I'd never seen anything like that before.

"They're adult movies," he explained. "Watch, you'll see how adults show love to each other."

Terrified he would think I was a child and not want to spend time with me anymore, I pretended it wasn't a big deal and sat there watching.

"Are you enjoying the movie?" he asked.

I shrugged and told him I didn't know.

"Let me touch you like that," he said. "You'll like it." His hand moved slowly up my inner thigh, his fingers gently stroking me as they moved upward and continued touching me where I knew his hand didn't belong. "Relax .Trust me," he said. "I want you to know how much I care about you." Embarrassed by my own ignorance, I didn't stop him. But he shouldn't have been touching me like that, or showing me that kind of movie. That much I knew.

From then on, I avoided Mike and never told anyone about that day. I would have been the one blamed anyway.

It was a few weeks later when Mike had seen me outside and cornered me. I tried to turn and walk away, but he grabbed hold of my arm.

"Wait," he said. "I just want to talk to you. How've you been? I haven't seen you lately. You okay?" I just nodded, but kept my eyes down. He asked me to lunch, but I said no. I had to go somewhere with my mother. "How about tomorrow?"

"I don't think I can." I shifted nervously from one foot to the

NEVER SAY NEVER

other, my eyes fixed on the concrete beneath them.

"You haven't said anything about our little secret have you?"

I looked at him for the briefest second, and then shook my head, no.

"That's good because they might not understand," he smiled. Try to come over as soon as you can because there's something I need to show you."

"What?"

"It's a surprise!"

"A surprise?" Curiosity won out and I agreed to see him later that afternoon.

When he came to the door, he sent me around back and told me he'd meet me there. I went without question.

"What's the surprise?" I asked from the doorway around back, excited to see what he had for me.

"Come in and I'll give it to you."

Inside, he had one reason after the other to delay. He even made sandwiches. We talked about why I hadn't come over to visit. Mike seemed genuinely disappointed.

"I miss our time together," he said. Then, he tried to kiss me. I was terrified he'd tell my parents and I'd catch a beating for even having been there, so I let him. Another one of Jack's beatings seemed so much worse than letting Mike kiss me. I'd quickly weighed it out in my mind, but when Mike started tugging at my clothing, trying to get it off, my fear barometer skyrocketed.

"Stop!" I yelled. "What are you doing? Stop it!" It was no use. My jeans were on the floor, my underwear tossed beside them. He shoved me down, pinning me against the floor with one hand, unbuttoning his jeans with the other. And then he climbed on top of me, forcing his manhood into me.

"Someday you'll understand." He buttoned his pants and straightened his shirt. "Until then, you'd better not tell anyone about our little time together. It wouldn't look good for you, now would it? I mean, you did come over here . . ."

I put my clothes on as fast as I could and got out of there without saying a word. It was getting dark outside and it was close to dinner time; I knew I'd better not be late. I walked home sobbing, but dried my eyes and swallowed the rest of my tears before walking into the house.

"You're late. Ten minutes. Where were you?" Mom asked.

"Out with friends."

"Where?"

"Just out," I shouted, and then quickly apologized before I got smacked.

"Go wash up and get ready to eat. Now!"

As I back to the kitchen, I thought about how not to get into trouble for what had just happened with Mike. With any luck, he wouldn't say a word and would never bother me again.

After dinner, I went to my room and collected everything Mike had ever given me. I marched outside and dumped it all in the trash. Then I got into the shower. I scrubbed and scrubbed, and then scrubbed again. No matter how many times I washed, it didn't feel like enough. I wondered if there was enough soap in the world.

Mike never bothered me again after that day. He went on with his life like it never happened. I went on with mine knowing it did.

CHAPTER SEVEN

Sal had lost his mind! "When you're of age you'll come and live with me," he'd said. "You can help around the house, clean, and I can teach you to cook for me, too."

I was stunned! And the expression on my face said exactly that. The man had gone around the curve and over the edge.

"Don't you want to live with me?"

"You're kidding, right?" How could he think . . .? He was the one who put me in foster care in the first place. And now that I was almost of age he could actually suggest that I would even consider moving in and taking care of him. Sure, I'll take care of him, just like he took care of me. Right!

"I have friends," I insisted. "I'm not leaving."

"Friends? You don't have any friends. You're going to live with me and that's final."

"Maybe I'll get married."

"Married? Why would you go and do a fool thing like that? You'd never be happy. Look what happened to your mother and me. She went and got sick, and stuck me with two kids to raise."

Sal's mind was set. Nothing I said made a difference. Once I was old enough, my job would be to care for him. It was actually pretty funny that he could think like that, but after all the money he paid to the state for of my so-called care, he thought he was entitled. I guess in his eyes, I owed him. That was one debt he'd never collect.

Once a year, Sal forced me to visit with his family at my grandmother's house in Brooklyn. The aunts, uncles, and cousins, would all be there and I would spend the entire day watching the group of parasites feed off of my grandmother. She had more money and heart than any of them. It didn't say too much for the group as a whole, but this was where my biological brother, Dan, had grown up. Needless to say, their collective wisdom had rendered my brother helpless and totally dependent on them. They, as a committee, had made all of Dan's decisions for him and he'd continued to allow them to do so, even beyond his eighteenth birthday.

My childhood may have been horrible, but at least it motivated me toward independence. Poor Dan never had a reason to get off the couch. Me, I knew life owed me nothing, but I was prepared to work hard and earn everything I wanted. In the long run, it seems I fared better than Dan. I may have come along second, but I was going to finish first.

CHAPTER EIGHT

The foster home where Tom had been moved was no longer able to care for him, so Tom came back to live with us again. I think it was the first time I ever had a prayer answered.

Dad didn't share my enthusiasm. Mom had to convince him it would only be for a little while, just until they could find a more permanent place for Tom.

It didn't take long, a few weeks at most, before Tom was getting into trouble again. The battles between Tom and Dad escalated, but there was nothing I could do except to stay out of the way. Tom could easily take care of himself now, although I did try to convince him to calm down and not go out of his way to stir Dad up. Unfortunately, anger had already gotten the best of Tom and there was no getting through to him.

One night, he came home late and Dad blew his cork big time. He went after Tom with a huge stick that he'd grabbed out of the front yard. Tom snatched that stick right out of Dad's hand and shot him a warning that even surprised me. "You touch me one more time old man and I'll take you down."

Tom meant it, too. His jaw was as rigid as a rock, and his eyes could've burned a hole right through Jack. Since Tom's six foot frame now towered over Dad's mere five-foot-five size, Dad backed off.

The two had sort of an understanding after that and stayed away from one another as much as possible. I tried to avoid Jack whenever possible, too. Mom started to keep her distance from him as well, especially since Jack's patience with her seemed to be wearing thin. She'd been setting him off as easily as we did. For the sake of survival, Mom learned to put some distance between them.

Mom and I finally had something in common and it worked to my advantage. Life had become a little more manageable since we were now on the same side. It wasn't the basis for a deep and lasting relationship, but it was something.

CHAPTER NINE

The tumultuous high school years were almost behind me, as I settled into my senior year with some pretty decent grades. My social life was beginning to pick up, too. That's when I met Robert. He was just home from Vietnam when we ended up at the same party.

"Has anyone ever told you that you look like Sophia Loren?" After that line I was in love! Robert had the nicest eyes, and was clearly taken with me. The interest was mutual. We dated for a while and soon were inseparable.

Dad liked Robert. He was always good about running little errands for Dad.

"Ask him to pick up a pack of cigarettes on his way over, will you?" Dad would say. And of course Robert was more than glad to do it.

Things seemed to settle down a bit at home, but at seventeen I was anxious to be done with school and move out of my house. It was so close to it happening. Finally, my hopes were becoming reality. I was so excited to start my life, to make my dreams come true, that I took five majors in order to graduate six months early.

Everything was going along just fine when my English teacher, for some odd reason, accused me of taking drugs. Here we go again, I thought.

After meeting with her, my mother asked me what the woman's problem was. What a turn of events! Mom never doubted me when it came to drugs; she knew I didn't take any. When faced with the accusation, she had no problem supporting me one-hundred-percent.

The next day, the teacher asked me to stay after class. I waited quietly for the venomous words that were sure to come.

"I spoke to your mother."

"Yes, I'm aware of that. She knows I don't do drugs."

"Well, if she believes that, then maybe the deeper problem is with her. Maybe she needs to be a better, more informed parent."

"Shut your mouth, witch, before I shut it for you." How odd it was to suddenly be defending the woman who had tormented me for years.

"You'll never amount to anything!" Suddenly, the teacher was clairvoyant. "Get out of my classroom. Get out of my sight."

After that I'd quickly turned my head when we passed each other in the hall. One day, she called out to me. "If you want to be as good as me, Celeste, you'll have to go a long way from where you are now. And quite frankly, I don't think you have the aptitude."

Clearly, it wasn't what you'd expect from a teacher and I just didn't have it in me to restrain myself. "Your life is so great?" I snarled. "Let me tell you, you made a big mistake accusing me. I may have problems, but drugs are not one of them. I don't know why you dislike me so much, but someday I'll show you just how wrong you were. And for the record, I don't want to be anything like you."

What her problem was I'll never know. I had turned my record around, was actually a good student, and never got into trouble anymore. Most of the teachers thought pretty highly of me. Still, I couldn't shake free of her hateful remarks.

I went to see Mrs. Hynds, a teacher whose insight I valued, hoping she could help me to let it go.

"Try not to take what she said to heart, dear. Always consider the source." Mrs. Hynds explained that there were situations I wasn't aware of, things she wasn't at liberty to speak about. She did, however, want me to know that the issue was with the teacher herself and not with me. Apparently, the administration was already involved in matters with the teacher, and they were already taking action to resolve those issues. It seemed that justice had been indirectly served. That would have to be enough for now.

NEVER SAY NEVER

Mrs. Hynds was the most inspiring of all my senior year teachers, planting seeds of courage inside of me. She declared I'd accomplish great things and that I had the strength to overcome anything. Compared to my past, I expected that the future would be a piece of cake.

Right before graduation she told me not to let anyone take me off course, that I had way too much promise for that. She also said that I should stay focused and I would succeed.

Once again, things had calmed down, but only briefly. Dad died in his sleep that year. He just went to bed one night and never got up the next day. Tom found him. He tried to do CPR, but it was no use; Dad was gone. Mom shooed me to my room as the police officers headed for hers, but I watched through a tiny crack in the doorway. I watched as the officer pulled the sheet over Dad's face.

That was when I barged into the room screaming, tears rolling. "Are you crazy? What are you doing? Leave him alone."

Tom draped an arm around my shoulders and tenderly nudged me out of the way. "It's going to be okay, Celeste. Everything is going to be okay."

Tom sat with me while I cried onto his shoulder, and then didn't object when I used his shirt to dry my face.

When the coroner was finished, his men wheeled Dad out on a gurney. His lifeless body was zipped into a black bag and straps were buckled across him. "Please let me see him. Don't take him yet," I pleaded with the attendants.

They waited while I leaned my head against Dad's chest. "I love you. I wish this wasn't happening. Really, I do."

Through all the beatings, all the ugly confrontations, the things he'd said and done; it was insane, but I was sorry he was gone.

"They have to leave now." Mom came up behind me and held my shoulders between her hands. I stood in the doorway and watched as they drove away. There were no sirens and no flashing lights. He was simply gone.

Mom closed the front door, turned the lock, and walked into the kitchen. She'd said I could stay home from school.

Mom made breakfast as if nothing had happened, and then went into her room and stripped the bed. From the closet, she pulled out fresh, brightly colored linens and dressed the bed with perfect creases and folds. I just watched, as she moved from one side of the bed to the other, tucking and straightening, without a hint of expression.

I was confused. How could I be so devastated over the death of a man I wished dead for so many years? Why should I be crying for him when he'd tortured me for years? It made no sense. I should have been celebrating.

Tom came from behind and put a hand on my shoulder. "Well, that's it. He's gone." Then, he turned and walked away.

I ran down the hall after him. "Tom? What's going on? Aren't you sad at all?"

"No. I hated the man. I'm actually glad he's gone."

His words didn't matter. I could see the truth. There was some sadness, even if he wasn't ready to admit to it.

How strange it was that I turned out to be the only one capable of expressing emotion.

CHAPTER TEN

Theresa was the likely choice to handle the funeral arrangements. Mom was still numb and Tom didn't care about the details. No one looked to me for help. Theresa was married, so she wasn't there when Dad passed. She'd always been Dad's favorite, the only one who had escaped his wrath. That could've been why she was so set on a proper and traditional burial, and so willing to handle it all.

Friends, family, and work associates came to the funeral home to say good-bye to Jack and pay their respects to us. Even Sal made an appearance.

Teary eyed and overwhelmed, I wanted to leave, but my mother needed me to be there with her. There must have been more than a hundred people over the course of the three day wake. Visitor after visitor shared memories of a man they couldn't have known very well. As it turned out, there were quite a few things my mother didn't know, either.

What a shock it was to find out Dad had often driven a woman home from work. "He was so kind," she'd said "He even loaned me money when I was short on my rent."

It was exasperating that he could be warm and wonderful to anyone other than his own family. How was it possible that we never knew that side of him?

Everyone talked about how wonderful he was.

"I can't count the times he paid for dinner. He was such a generous man!" a different woman said.

Apparently, he was quite the ladies man.

"He was so personable and charming. He had a way about him

you just couldn't resist. All the ladies at work just adored him," a third woman said.

My mother thanked each one for their kind words, but I knew it broke her heart to hear them. I swallowed hard, thankful he never pretended to love me.

"What's wrong?" Sal asked.

"Excuse me? In case you hadn't noticed, my father just died."

"So? You never liked him anyway. What's the problem?"

My expression turned sour at his words. "If you can't behave in public, then just go home." That man was impossible. I walked away from him, as if denying any connection at all.

Sal paid his respects to my mother, and then took a seat in the back row. I had no tolerance for such a pathetic excuse for a human being.

It was hardly a blip in time and life resumed. Rob proposed and I accepted. Senior year was almost finished and I had my heart set on going to college. Rob objected, but I knew a college education was the only way I could do something worthwhile with my life, so I continued to plead my case. After all, what kind of job would I get without one? No one in Rob's family or in mine was willing to support my plan for college, not even my mother. For the time being I had to let it go.

After some time had gone by, I tried again. "Forget it! We'll be married soon and I'll be taking care of you, and you'll be taking care of our family." He wasn't angry, just set with a plan of his own.

Sal showed up again, disgruntled over the engagement, insisting that after I graduated my place was with him.

Mom was finally showing signs of life again, growing closer to both Tom and me. Finally, we were a family, the three of us. She was taking an active interest in our lives and futures, just like a real mother. When she offered to help with my wedding plans, I kissed her on the cheek and said of course. There was no need for grudges. It was time to celebrate the life that was just beginning.

One day, not long before graduation, Mom asked if we could talk. She brought two steamy mugs of coffee to the table and motioned for me to join her.

"I know it was difficult for you," she said, as she poured a little milk into each cup. "I mean your life here."

I took a sip.

"But I wanted you to know that I always cared about you and no matter what it seemed like, I never wanted you to get hurt."

"Then why did you let Jack treat me that way?"

"He wasn't always a mean man." Her eyes searched the well worn floor tiles. "I was pregnant after Theresa was born. The baby died during delivery. It was a boy. Jack never forgave me and he was never the same after that."

"Why did you stay with him then?"

"Divorce wasn't an option for me. I didn't need people staring and talking behind my back. Besides, where would I go and who would support me?"

I lashed out. "You should have left him. He didn't deserve you, and you certainly deserved better than the likes of him."

"There were foster children before you . . . without incident."

"My life was a living hell! And you let it happen. Why couldn't you stop him? He beat us over and over again." It all came out; the intensity building from years of abuse, years of pain.

"I'm so sorry. Very sorry for all of it, but I was afraid. Afraid he would leave or what he would have done to me if he hadn't."

Now it was my eyes that searched the floor. There in the kitchen, on that very day, I discovered the truth . . . she had been as helpless as I was.

We finished our coffee in silence.

CHAPTER ELEVEN

The graduation ceremony was over and I held up my diploma as Mom snapped another picture. We all out went out to eat in honor of the occasion. It was the first party, I realized, that had ever been given for me.

Eighteen, it turned out, not only marked the end of my high school years, but the end of the state's interest in my life. It was another cause for celebration. The only drawback was that Mom no longer received payments for my living expenses. I had to find a job, fast.

Rob, only recently having been discharged from the army, didn't have a job yet. In the meantime, his parents were supporting him. He didn't seem very motivated to find work, but as the understanding bride-to-be, I assumed he just needed a little more time to adjust to being back. Sooner or later, I was sure he would find something.

It was unfortunate that I didn't connect the dots and see the picture that was forming. Not only was Rob in no hurry to get a job, he didn't even show any desire to get a driver's license. He was content to have me chauffer him around, or take the bus. It would have taken effort to convert his military driver's license to a civilian one. The pattern, it seemed, had already been established and I'd been too blind to notice.

On the other hand, I found the act of job hunting to be exhilarating. The prospect of being valued for something I did was absolutely incredible. And then to get paid for it, too! That was the attitude that got me hired. I landed a great job in Manhattan, working for an accounting firm.

My life officially began to take shape and over the course of a few years, I put myself through an evening program and earned my college degree. But nothing had ever changed for Rob. He still lacked ambition and I'd had my doubts before marrying him. "Get a job or the wedding's off," I threatened on more than one occasion.

Amazingly enough, Rob became a corporate trader at a brokerage house in Manhattan, thanks to a friend who'd gotten him the interview. Between the job and the commute, Rob was suddenly a busy man. Unfortunately, it was all too fast and too much for him. He had difficulty adapting to the daily stress and started to drink after work.

"It's all part of the politics," he claimed. "Everyone goes out after work, even the senior partners." But soon enough, the drinking became a problem. Intoxicated, he'd call me at all hours of the night, belligerent and nasty, and then he had no recollection the next morning, just acted like nothing happened.

"I'm thinking of calling the wedding off," I announced.

"Fine if that's the way you want it."

It had been a short phone call, but a necessary one. I had serious doubts about marrying an unmotivated man with a drinking problem. It seemed like a recipe for disaster. One of the senior partners at my firm had noticed I was upset. He asked if there was anything he could do.

"No, thank you. It was just a misunderstanding with my fiancé."

"Would you like to talk about it?"

"Not really." But I was so upset I couldn't concentrate and he could see that.

"C'mon," he offered. "Let's go get some lunch. Some fresh air may just do the trick."

Reluctant at first, I nodded in agreement, slid open my desk drawer, and grabbed my purse.

Art was very understanding and having been married for quite some time, he was able to share some wisdom.

"Celeste, if you're having problems now, perhaps its best to reconsider the idea of marriage to this man. If you don't mind my saying so, you're a very pretty young woman who should have no

NEVER SAY NEVER

trouble finding someone else."

"Thank you, Art. And yes, I'm giving serious thought to calling off the wedding."

The fresh air and nice lunch had worked. I was tired of thinking and talking about Rob, so I asked Art to tell me a little about his family. He wasn't very open and attempted to switch the subject very quickly. He was evasive, but not rude. What he wanted to discuss was my appearance. He obviously was taken with it. I hadn't had much experience fielding compliments, but I did my best to receive his kind words, but also tried to change the subject.

We walked slowly back to the office, enjoying the warmth of the day, when I noticed Rob was waiting in front of the building. Art excused himself and made his way inside.

"What are you doing with him?" he asked.

"We had lunch."

"You had lunch with a man?" His finger was far too close to my face, as he spoke.

"That was my boss." Rob turned berry red, yelling with a foul mouth.

I'd tolerated years of abuse and I wasn't about to take any from Rob. I looked him squarely in the eye and told him to go back to his office. Then, I turned and walked away. Obscenities spewed from behind me, but my dignity remained intact. His, however, seemed to be diminishing fast.

I was hardly surprised when Rob called later that evening to apologize. He wanted to meet and talk it out. Reluctantly, I agreed and the following evening we had dinner. Fool that he was, Rob ordered a drink and I didn't stop him. Naturally, it didn't take long for him to become verbally abusive, so I drove him straight home, dropped him at the curb and went home.

The next day, there was another phone call and another apology. "It's just pre-wedding jitters. That's all it is. We're both nervous."

I lowered my voice to a level of quiet control and warned, "You had better think before you act because I am not going to tolerate this kind of nonsense. I'm done with that, Rob. Do you understand?" Then, I did the unthinkable. I forgave him.

CHAPTER TWELVE

I should've seen it as an omen. It was supposed to be the greatest day of my life and it was raining.

"Celeste, you look lovely." My mother's eyes watered.

"Mom, c'mon, you'll ruin your make-up."

"Promise me you won't get pregnant right away. Wait and make sure you're both ready before you bring a child into the marriage. You've been arguing a lot lately. I'm just a little concerned, that's all. If you change your mind, having a child would only complicate the situation."

My mind flashed to how she just watched while Jack would beat me. Now, she was worried about me?

She must have seen the perplexed look on my face. She took my hand in hers. "You were a terror, Celeste, but I always loved you. I know I can't change the past and I am truly sorry, but I can do something about the future, about now. Don't jump into this marriage if you're not sure. You can stay with me as long as you want. There's no hurry."

Where was this woman all my life, I wondered. She shows up on my wedding day, ready to become a mother now that I don't need one anymore. I swallowed both the anger and the laughter that were rising in my throat.

"Mom, I love him. He's good to me. Believe it or not, we're going to have a normal life. And after everything I've been through, don't you think I deserve that? Please be happy for me."

"Of course, I am, but I can't help worrying. Is he really the one for you? I'm just trying to protect you. Yes, I know it's a little late, but better late than not at all."

I couldn't hold back any longer. The peace we'd made just a short time ago, now forgotten. The pain was too deep, had festered so long. It poured out in a deluge. "You never cared before. Was it the money? How could you . . ." And then I stopped, mid-sentence. No, not on my wedding day; I wasn't going to do this.

"How dare you judge me?" she snapped. I'd wounded her. "I loved children. All of my life I wanted a big family. There were so many miscarriages, and then I couldn't conceive; that's why I became a foster mother."

"Your husband was an animal," I fought back. "He made me feel like nothing, less than dirt; neither one of you ever cared anything about me or my future. And now, today of all days, you think you can be the mother you never were? Protect me? I needed your protection then. I don't need it now." My rainy day wedding had turned into an unexpected storm.

"Listen to me. When I was a young girl my parents didn't take any interest in my future. I was one of ten children. Do you think my parents had time to ask each one us how we felt about anything? But even so, I still knew they loved me."

"I bet your father never beat you."

"Yes, actually he did. When we were bad, Daddy would take off his belt and give it to us good. So, you see, I do know what it feels like."

"Why are you telling me all this now? Are you purposely trying to ruin my wedding?"

"Of course not. I just want to make sure you're not making a mistake; doing something for the wrong reason."

Just then, Theresa walked in. "What's going on in here?" Her accusation was directed at me. To her, I was always the cause of whatever was going on. "Why is my mother so upset?"

"Ask her," I pointed across the room, accusingly, to the woman who was professing to care. "And if you don't mind, discuss it somewhere else. I need to finish my make-up. I am getting married today, you know."

"It wasn't always so bad for you," Mom continued as if Theresa had never interrupted. "We took you to Florida, other places, too." Theresa stood there, silently watching as we hashed out old wounds. "Not everyone gets to go on vacation. Maybe your memory is conveniently selective. There was some good you know."

"Not nearly enough to balance the scale! As if anything could." I stormed out of the room, seething, as layers of crinoline, satin, and lace scraped against the wall. I turned back with one last word. "The only reason you took us with you is because no one would watch us. The trips were for you, never me. Everything was for you. You never cared about me; you were paid for the job you did."

The limousine pulled up to the house twenty minutes later. The driver held the door and without a word between us, Theresa, Mom, and I slid in.

Theresa's husband was far more gracious than she had ever been. Freddy walked me down the aisle, my beaded arm resting on his tuxedoed sleeve. He'd been the closest thing to a father I'd ever had, the only person I could talk openly with and trust not to betray me. Kind and considerate, he was the obvious choice to give me away. I smiled at the memory of how he'd warned Rob that he'd answer to him if he ever hurt me.

Sal had never even been a consideration to give the bride away. I didn't even invite him to the wedding.

Rob stood by the altar, waiting to receive his bride. His eyes sparkled like stars in the night and my heart fluttered with expectation. I held tightly onto the white rose bouquet draped over my hand, as Freddy gently lifted my veil and kissed my cheek. Rob took the few steps to where I stood and offered his hand to me. My breath caught as we touched.

"We are gathered here today in the presence of God, family, and friends . . ." Father McDowell smiled as he completed the ceremony, pronouncing us husband and wife.

The music played as Rob and I made our way up the aisle to form a receiving line, and then it was on to the reception.

Tables were set with crisp white linens, centerpieces overflowed with flowers, and servers folded napkins again and again throughout the evening. We danced and ate, and then danced some more. I was the center of attention; finally, the star of my own life.

My mother apologized for what had happened earlier and she wished me all the happiness in the world. "Remember," she said, "I love you."

Rob and I stayed overnight in a hotel and the next morning were off to honeymoon in Aruba. The food, the ocean, it was all so incredible. But after spending a little too much time outdoors, I ended up with sun poisoning. I insisted Rob go down to the casino and have some fun, but when he came back to the room he was drunker than drunk. His foul mouth was flaring, accusing me of spoiling our honeymoon. Although it was true, I was reasonably sure it was not something a groom should be saying to his new bride.

The next morning he woke up bright and cheery, as though nothing had happened.

"Rob, you weren't very nice last night. Why were you so nasty when you came back to the room?"

His eyes scrunched into a look of obvious confusion. "I wasn't nasty," he insisted, baffled by the insanity of my accusation.

I could feel my eyebrows rise and let the subject drop there. It had no chance of ending on a good note. Feeling a little better after a full night's sleep, I was back to myself. Careful to avoid getting sun, Rob and I went sightseeing, gambled, and then enjoyed a romantic dinner.

Everything was forgotten and we were the happy newlyweds again, at least until it was time to check-out. The front desk attendant handed Rob the bill and after looking it over he casually blurted out that he didn't have the money to pay for it.

"What do you mean you don't have money? How could you not have money? That's ridiculous!" I argued. "I paid for most of the wedding. You were responsible for the honeymoon. I don't understand. Rob, what's going on?"

NEVER SAY NEVER

It was inconceivable that he could stand there without a hint of shame and declare he couldn't pay the bill. Talk about mortified!

To make matters worse, I'd left my credit cards home. Why would I need to bring them if my husband was there to pay? How embarrassing that Rob had to call his brother to bail us out of the situation.

We hardly exchanged two words the entire way to the airport, but once we had checked in and were awaiting take-off, I finally had to bring it up again. "I don't understand how you could take me on a honeymoon and not bring money to pay the bill. It's unthinkable. How could you embarrass us like that?"

"I didn't bring a lot of money and wasn't sure how much everything would cost."

"That's a reason to bring more, not less." I wanted to leave him right then and there. Thank heaven we were on the plane or I would have.

As if I hadn't already suffered enough humiliation, when we landed at Kennedy Airport we didn't have the cab fare to get home. Again, Rob called his brother; this time to pick us up.

CHAPTER THIRTEEN

Married life began frugally in the basement apartment of my mother's house. Rob and I had redecorated and had agreed to split the cost.

My contributions were already in place. One of Rob's, the console television, was being delivered the next day. Rob was at work, but I had the rest of the week off and planned to be home for the delivery.

"It's C.O.D., Ma'am." The driver handed me a bill.

"Are you sure? My husband paid for this already. There has to be some mistake."

I called the store and they confirmed there was a balance due. Then, I called Rob.

"I didn't have the money to pay in full," he explained.

"You could have mentioned it instead of letting me get caught by surprise. Forget it. We'll talk later," I said.

I gave the guy a check and an apology. He gave me the television and a sympathetic look.

Rob waltzed in at the end of the day ready to do battle. He grabbed a couple of tall boys from the frig, and then we went to war. In the end, I crawled into bed exhausted and defeated.

My dream marriage had turned into a nightmare. Then, it got worse. Rob discovered the bar car on the Long Island Railroad.

Getting back to work was a relief, something to focus my attention on other than my disastrous life. But it seemed Art now had a personal agenda. Every day I declined his invitations: lunch, dinner, and assorted excursions under the guise of business. Eventually, he tired of asking and fired me.

With hardly any lag time, I was hired by a freight forwarding company on the grounds of Kennedy Airport. My brother-in-law had heard about the opening and I sent a resume. One short interview later, I had the job.

My new commute was only a twenty minute drive, saving me money and time from traveling to the city. From the start, I was trained in the fine art of Japanese business customs. They held to a strict code of ethics and all employees were expected to maintain that standard. Their culture dictated that customers were to be treated as if they were royalty.

"We are servants to our customers. They are kings," I was told by the vice-president on more than one occasion. "In this company we are honored to have been chosen to serve them. To have a career with us, you must adopt our philosophy."

With a mounting stack of bills and an unreliable husband at home, I embraced their policy with fervor. It really wasn't that hard to grasp—without a customer there is no business.

Like a sponge, I absorbed every necessary detail in order to get ahead. It paid off, too. I was promoted from a sales position to management, overseeing several departments. Now I was somebody.

It took five years to realize their increasing profit margin was not going to be shared among the employees. While my salary hardly changed, the demands of the job increased dramatically. As I became well versed in International Law, I turned into a personal assistant, legal council, or whatever was needed at the moment.

Trainees were routinely brought over from Japan to learn the American way. They were here on four year visas and we were responsible for their welfare during that time. It was a shame that one of the first American practices learned was driving under the influence of alcohol.

Naturally, the responsibility to represent them in court fell to me. I'd learned enough Japanese to act as liaison in these situations, handling immigration and reporting directly to the head office. But keeping these recruits out of trouble had become a full time job. One

NEVER SAY NEVER

I did not want.

I'd finally had enough and tendered my resignation. Offers flew onto the table, but it was too late. The time for compensation had long passed. I'd been searching for another job and found one, so with a handshake and great sadness we parted company.

CHAPTER FOURTEEN

My new job came with a nice big hike in pay. I was now the Operations Manager at another freight forwarding company. With the increased income, Rob and I were able to afford a home of our own. We searched Queens and eventually expanded the search to Long Island. Finally, we found it, a two family brick home with six rooms up and five down. It was a beautiful corner lot on a tree lined street in Bay Shore, not too far from the water.

Mom was ready to sell her house anyway, so the timing was right. Theresa had offered Mom a place with her and Teddy. Mom was thrilled. She'd be living rent free.

With the new job came a longer commute and a lot more hours at the office, but it suited me fine. I was able to avoid Rob who'd been coming home nastier than ever. My feelings for him were slowly diminishing along with my patience. No matter how many times I insisted he stop drinking, he didn't. His defense was that his friends all drank and their wives didn't have a problem with it. In his own mind, he was as normal as anyone else. Considering he never remembered his tirades, it was impossible to show him any different.

I went to Mom and Theresa for help, but they only saw Rob the entertainer. He was always the perfect host, making jokes for his audience. When everyone went home he would become an uncontrollable, foul-mouthed drunk. Since they'd never witnessed that side of him, they insisted I was just unstable and looking for a way out of the marriage.

"You have a perfectly good husband," they both defended. "He's a good man. Besides, Rob's parents have agreed to sell their house and rent the downstairs apartment in your beautiful new home, just to help you with the mortgage. Marriage is for better or worse, Celeste. Learn how to get along."

It was disheartening that no one knew the truth. At least when we all moved into the new house, my in-laws were able to see for themselves what was going on with their son. They sympathized with me and did their best to help, but there was nothing they could really do.

Rob's drinking was out of control. "I'm leaving unless you get help," I threatened.

He laughed, but knew I meant business. I hoped it would be enough.

It wasn't long after that when Rob came home late from a business dinner. I'd been watching from the window as he fell out of the cab, head first onto the sidewalk. Then, he made his way up the front walk and crawled upstairs.

Between the sight and smell, I just tore into him. "If you don't stop drinking, I swear I'm going to leave you."

"Go ahead. I don't need you. See if somebody else will take you because I could care less." Spit flew with every hateful word. His arm was cocked and ready to swing when he lost his balance and stumbled to the floor. It gave me just enough time and space to grab a pillow and head for the couch downstairs.

The next morning before work, I knocked on the bathroom door. "Rob, we have to talk."

Wearing a big smile, he opened the door. His arms were fully extended and ready to wrap around me.

I took a step back. "I'm done, Rob. I'm not putting up with this nonsense another second. Get yourself some help or you'll never be anything other than a no good drunk."

"I . . . I'm sorry," he said with his head hung low. "I swear I'll stop this time, for good. It'll never happen again. I swear it on my life."

"Your life's not worth much at the moment. You say that every time and it's always the same thing. I've had it. I deserve better and I'm going to get it."

NEVER SAY NEVER

His eyes started to well and my heart broke for him, but I had to remain strong. He was a prisoner to the alcohol, trying to overcome the nightmares of Vietnam. He'd never admit it, but I knew he struggled with the horrors he'd seen. Sober, he was the man I loved, but the abusive drunk had to go.

I went to work and cried the entire day. Leaving was the right answer and seemed so simple when I'd said it, but I loved him and it was hard to let go of the dream I'd had for us. And what would I do with the in-laws? They'd been kind to a fault, but they couldn't do a thing to stop Rob from drinking. No one could.

My in-laws were the most giving and loving people I'd ever known. My father-in-law called me kitten, which always made me smile. He would give us his last dime if we needed it. And their marriage was the kind I'd always dreamed of having. Dad had his flaws, especially the card playing. Sometimes he'd lose more than they could afford, but Mom would get up and make his breakfast anyway, dedicated and loving, not a trace of anger.

I'd take her out for brunch once in a while and buy her little gifts to show her how much she meant to me, but she'd always return the gift and tell me to save the money. The woman did for everyone: cooked, sewed, cleaned, you name it, and there was hardly a thank you ever passed from anyone's lips. It just wasn't right.

One day I approached my father-in-law. "Mom saw a coat she really liked. Why don't you surprise her with it?"

My heart wanted desperately to see her face light up with joy, even if only for a moment.

"She already has one," he protested. "It'd be a waste of money." He didn't understand. It wasn't about practicality but showing her how valued she was. It was something I had always wanted to feel. Now, I wanted it for her.

"You've got to be kidding! Her coat is twenty-years-old, at least. She deserves something new. Instead of gambling your money away, why not spend some of it on Mom."

Once the words had left my mouth, I knew I'd gone too far. His eyes burned into me, but he didn't say a thing. He turned his head away, back to the newspaper. I had inadvertently crossed a boundary and been exiled as a result.

Frustrated, I stormed out of the room. I wanted to buy her the coat myself and would have, too, but Rob and I didn't have the money at the moment.

Dad must have given it some more thought. The following week he took Mom to get a new coat. Afterward, they went out for a nice lunch.

CHAPTER FIFTEEN

Whether it was my ultimatum, red eyes, or listless attitude, Rob was convinced I was leaving him this time, and his drinking actually slowed down. I didn't discuss it after that, but continued to stay alert for signs of his backsliding.

Things were somewhat stable for the time being, so I was able to focus on my career. I'd already established some solid business connections and developed a few close friendships. Astonishingly, one of those relationships turned into a partnership. Dave's trucking company was expanding and he needed help. He was looking for someone who could manage the drivers as well as handle the books, a person he could trust.

"It's not that I wouldn't love to do it," I said, "but I just don't have the money to buy in."

"That's not a problem, Celeste. I've got money. What I need is a partner. It's too much for one person and I don't know who else could handle the job, and not cut my throat in the process."

"Dave, I know we'd be successful, but I'd have to pull my own weight. I can't accept charity."

"I could structure the deal in a way that you could pay me off a little each week."

"If you're serious, it could work." I thought about the implications of a full partnership. "Well, Rob and I would finally be able to start a family."

"Celeste, with us teaming up, you'll be able to afford a huge family."

"Draw up the papers. You've got yourself a deal."

CHAPTER SIXTEEN

Confident in the success of my new partnership, there was nothing stopping Rob and I from starting a family, but we were disappointed when six months had passed and I still wasn't pregnant. Fighting discouragement, I'd made an appointment to see the doctor.

"I don't understand why I haven't been able to conceive. Do you think there's something wrong with me, Doctor?"

"You said it's only been a few months since you've started trying? Isn't that correct?"

"Yes, but I know plenty of people who get pregnant right away."

"Well, some do, but most don't. We can certainly run some tests to rule out infertility. Hopefully, that will put your mind at ease."

The testing revealed an obstruction. Surgery was scheduled for the following week. With that behind us, Rob and I resumed trying. Two months later I was back in the doctor's office, this time for back pain and nausea.

After a urine test and examination the nurse seated me in front of the doctor's desk. I was a wreck, as I waited for the results. It was one thing after another and I couldn't bear any more bad news.

"Hmm," The doctor's brows furrowed, as he walked in reading my chart. He seated himself and looked directly at me, pausing before he spoke.

"Am I sick? Dying? What's wrong?" I snapped.

He shuffled through a couple of pages from my chart. "From the looks of these results, I'd say you're pregnant. Congratulations," he looked at me and smiled.

I don't think my feet touched the floor for the rest of the day.

"A grandchild!" Dad was close to tears when I told him. Dad was the only one home, so I phoned everyone else as fast as I could, one right after the other.

Rob was elated.

Dave cried.

My mother was happy, but worried again.

Now, with a baby on the way, I was more determined than ever that the business was going to be a huge success. I began putting in longer hours than I had before. This child of mine was going to have an incredible future filled with everything money could buy. I was going to make sure he would never want for anything.

As my belly grew, Rob continued to drink moderately. Things were good until my eighth month, when I'd come home earlier than usual to prepare a nice dinner. Rob hadn't expected me to be there and he walked in half-drunk. "We're out of beer," he said, as he rummaged through the refrigerator.

"And?"

"Get me some."

Still without a driver's license, he depended on rides from the rest of us. His brother drove him to the train every morning, and his father and I took turns with everything else. Just the thought made me crazy. I'd argued with him so many times . . . "You need to get your license." Eventually, I stopped bringing the subject up because it only triggered his anger.

Avoiding unnecessary vulgarity seemed prudent at the time, so when dinner was in the oven and the timer set, I drove him to the store. But later I paid a higher price. The rest of the evening declined rapidly, his belligerence rising along with his blood alcohol level. He refused to eat dinner and followed me downstairs when I had finished mine.

"Leave me alone!" I cried out.

His mother was sitting next to me and she had also become irritated with him. She yelled at him to stop, but he didn't appreciate that and put his hand on her shoulder and pushed. I screamed for him to stop. Rob didn't take too kindly to that and lunged at me. I hurried my pregnant self down the hall and up the stairs as fast as I could, but it wasn't fast enough. Rob grabbed the back of my shirt just before I cleared the bedroom doorway. He took a swing, but missed. I'd tried to duck, lost my balance, and fell onto the floor. He lifted his foot off the ground, ready to kick, but his mother had come up behind us and grabbed him just in time.

"Leave her alone!" She'd caught him by surprise and he lost his balance. He fell onto the bed and it looked like he'd passed out.

With her help, I managed to lift myself off the floor, and then we slipped downstairs as quietly as we could. Not a single word was uttered by either one of us. We just sat on the couch, clinging to one another.

Rob's brother, Peter, had come home a few minutes later. He took one look at the two of us and raced up the stairs two at a time. We heard the squeal of bed springs as Peter undoubtedly pulled his brother from the bed. Threats spewed and before punches could be thrown, I waddled up the steps..

"Stop it right now or I'll call the police." Mom was only seconds behind me and I had to act fast before she got hurt.

"Mom, go downstairs, please. I don't want them knocking into you."

"You're eight months pregnant; Celeste. I'm not leaving you alone in the middle of this."

Peter took a step back to give us a chance to get out of the way, but instead of leaving, I said, "Mom, I love you. Please take Peter downstairs, so I can try to get Rob to bed. Our only hope is if he sleeps it off. He'll be okay in the morning. He always is. You know that."

"No," my brother-in-law insisted. " You go and take a ride or something. Get out of the house and let me settle him down."

"Please, Celeste, think of the baby," my mother-in-law pleaded.

Reluctantly, I picked up my purse and jacket, and left the two of them to deal with Rob. Forty-five minutes later, I called from a payphone at the gas station to see what was going on. They were worried about me, but I assured them I was fine.

Sitting in the car I realized just how mad I was. If I hadn't been pregnant I would have beaten the living hell out of him. And I could have, too.

Rob and I often joked about the time we were at a bar and he'd gotten a little too rambunctious. From behind, he'd wrapped his forearm around my neck. He thought he had me in a good headlock, but I surprised the both of us when I flipped him over my shoulder and sent him barreling through the door, head first into a parked car.

He never knew I'd taken self defense classes after Dad died. I'd paid close attention and worked hard, practicing to get it right. For me, being able to defend myself had become as important as breathing.

CHAPTER SEVENTEEN

Our son, Keith Michael, was born on August 09, 1979. Rob had calmed down that last month before Keith arrived, and everything seemed to be going well. As grateful as I was for a healthy baby and a calm home, the bills soon began to pile up and Rob was not going to be the one to pick up the slack. It was inevitable the day would come and I'd have to refocus myself again.

Thank heaven for my mother-in-law. She was delighted to watch Keith and on a few occasions, my foster mother helped out, too. All seemed to be transitioning well until Rob started drinking excessively, again. Suddenly, he decided the baby should be in bed when he came home from work. Tending to Keith seemed to interfere with Rob's relaxation time. Unfortunately, the way my schedule was less than predictable, many nights I didn't walk through the door before eight o'clock. So it became Rob's responsibility to take care of Keith at those times. Of course the imposition wreaked havoc on our marriage, and the constant battles took a toll, especially on the baby.

By the time Keith was six-months-old, he'd be flinching and screaming as the two of us went at it. I was beside myself. Keith was suffering and it seemed all it took to set Rob off was my presence. Not knowing what else to do to avoid the arguments, I stayed overnight with friends and started thinking about divorce.

Before I knew what'd happened, I ended up in the arms of Larry, a man I'd met at a restaurant near my office. Larry appreciated me and brought laughter back to my life. He was a welcome and timely gift. Talking for hours, sharing secret parts of ourselves, it was inevitable we'd fall in love.

Once in a while, I'd steel myself for battle and go home. It was still an impossible situation and the day finally came when I knew I was finished.

After food shopping, I'd asked Rob to watch the baby and change him while I put the groceries away. When he refused, the argument began and quickly escalated until Keith was screaming and trembling in my arms.

This was no life for any of us. My eight-month old son was inconsolable and I was on the verge of a breakdown. I asked my mother-in-law to watch the baby, so I could get out and calm myself down. I handed Keith to her, and then grabbed a big black bag, stuffing as much as I could fit into it: slacks, tops, shoes . . . Mom and Dad would take care of Keith for the night; I was certain of that. But instead of going back the next day, I went to my mother's house and told her what had been going on. Now that Keith was involved she listened, but still sent me back home.

In the meantime, my only solace was Larry. He and I continued to see each other, building a strong bond as we navigated the details of our individual lives. His story, as it turned out, was more complicated than mine since his financial future rested on his upcoming marriage to the boss' daughter. That kind of security was hard to walk away from.

For me it was simple. I slipped out of the family one day at time. Eventually, I was only there on weekends. Since my mother was too old to take responsibility for Keith it made sense for him to stay where he was. It wasn't the perfect arrangement, but it seemed to be the only reasonable choice at the moment.

Rob's mother continued to watch Keith during the day, and then Rob would take over after work. Suddenly, he was capable of doing the right thing. I wondered where he'd been the whole time I was there.

Rob called often, pleading with me to come home. He promised again and again he'd stop drinking, but it was too late. I'd learned that a desperate man will say just about anything. Besides, both Rob and his empty words meant nothing to me anymore.

My father-in-law was heartbroken. I didn't blame him when he turned his back on me. Though his son was to blame, it was hard for him to understand how a woman could leave her husband and child. Ironically, I often wondered the very same thing.

CHAPTER EIGHTEEN

The divorced years turned into good ones. Each of us took a part in Keith's life, and yet we were all able to move forward in our own. With free time on my hands now, I volunteered for the Auxiliary Police. I found it fulfilling to be part of a uniformed patrol which helped to ensure the safety of the community.

When the holidays came around I'd spend them with Rob, Keith and the in-laws, playing the part of a devoted family member. Larry spent the holidays with his fiancé and her family. It was necessary to keep up appearances or risk losing his standing in the family and company. As strange as it sounds, it wasn't a bad arrangement. Keith got the family time he deserved, and Larry did what he had to do.

Rob's brother moved to Minnesota and Rob met Jane during one of his visit's there. Eventually, Jane came to New York, married Rob, and moved into our house. Unfortunately, since I wouldn't agree to an annulment, Jane couldn't have the church wedding she'd wanted. How sad for Jane.

Knowing that Rob would never be able to provide for Keith, work always remained my first priority. I was determined that my son would have everything he needed, and lots more.

Larry eventually married his fiancé, but it didn't really change much for us. With business thriving the way it was, I didn't have time to pursue or cultivate a new relationship, so the arrangement worked just fine for me. The fact that Larry's marriage soon ended in divorce was no great surprise. But the discussion of a possible marriage between us was. It didn't strike me as a fabulous idea, so we just kept things the way they were.

Once the wrong pieces of my life had been cut away, it was easier to value the right ones. Larry and I saw each other whenever possible, and Keith spent much of that time with us. My life had come together, finally. I was a successful business woman, mother, and had found a wonderful man.

Sometimes business would take Larry across the country for weeks at a time. Normally, it wasn't a problem for either of us, but this time he'd been experiencing bouts of pain in his lower abdomen. That concerned me. He'd seen a doctor who attributed it to the added stress, poor eating habits, and irregular sleep patterns due to the traveling. He suggested that once Larry was back on a normal routine the situation would correct itself. But following his return, weeks had passed and Larry didn't seem to be improving. The pain medication wasn't helping, and one night the pain became so intense that I had to rush Larry to the hospital.

After testing, the doctor gave us the news. "I'm sorry, but there's a tumor in Larry's intestines."

The ugly green walls seemed to close in on me and the smell of disinfectant became so strong I nearly gagged. It had to be a mistake, some sort of bad dream. Weakness overcame my legs and I reached for a chair.

Doctor after doctor, treatment after treatment . . . surgery, radiation, and chemo all proved useless. Larry just got sicker and sicker. And then the phone call came.

"Celeste, you need to come. Larry's failing," the nurse's voice was soft, but urgent.

I ran nine red lights, but made it. Taking Larry's hand, I vowed to love him for all eternity. When his fingers gently slipped from mine, I knew I'd lost the love of my life.

CHAPTER NINETEEN

Grief had stolen three years from my life as well as added forty pounds to my frame. Larry was gone and I was devastated. Unable to cope with life, I'd sold my thirty-five percent of the business back to Dave and buried myself in food and drink.

Limited as to what I was ready to handle, I chose to go back into sales. Working for another freight forwarding company was where I'd met Ted. He was extremely influential, well connected, and there at just the right time in my life. Of course, he was married. Since my focus on a relationship would always have to come second to my career, marital status was not a huge deterrent. I was entertainment for him and he was a distraction for me. It was another perfect relationship. Especially since his money flowed like a fountain, and a lot of it went in my direction.

Over the next year, my emotions shifted back into place and I was ready to leave my job in order to pursue something more profitable. Between what I'd made from selling my shares back to Dave and what I'd been able to tuck away, there was plenty for a new venture.

The market looked good, so I took a chance and purchased a commercial property. It wasn't the best choice for an investment, but as luck would have it, in two years I was out with a nice return.

Now that I had my own flowing fountain, Ted's money no longer interested me. He'd also lost the ability to distract me, so that was the end of that relationship. But as the empty space inside of me grew, so did my appetite. Then, completely frustrated with myself, I drank to release the pressure of those feelings. It seemed that was my cycle for healing. Thank goodness I had my one saving grace, Keith.

I would never let him down and so I always found my way back to life, back to the job, and back to the money trail.

It was easiest to push off from air freight sales and it seemed I never had a problem finding work. So that's what I did, got back into the daily grind of business and left soaking my sorrows for the weekend.

One night, I just happened to be in the right place at the right time and there she was, my old English teacher. I knew the day would come . . . Memories of how she condemned me to a life of failure burned in my gut, anger rose like bile in my throat.

Like a cat after prey, I inched my way over. "Hi, remember me?"

"Should I?" she asked.

"I'm Celeste . . . I was one of your students."

"How are you, Celeste? It's nice to see you again."

"Unfortunately, I can't say the same."

"Excuse me?" Her eyebrows lifted.

"Do you remember your prediction?"

"No. I'm afraid I don't know what you're referring to."

"You said I'd never amount to anything. And you were so certain of it, too. Looks like you were wrong. Apparently, you never turned out to be anything other than a working class teacher. Me, I'm in air freight, and I dabble in commercial real estate, as well. Did you see the Porsche out front? Well, it's mine. You probably still drive that old bucket of rust. You always did have one clunker or another. Poor thing, trying to survive on a teacher's salary."

I tossed a hundred dollar bill onto the bar. "Have one on me." I smiled, and headed for the door.

CHAPTER TWENTY

"The gentleman over there would like to buy you a drink." The bartender said, as he pointed toward the end of the bar.

Well, the night was about to get interesting. "Vodka tonic, and make it Grey Goose while you're at it. On second thought, hold the tonic."

The first sip was like a moonlit promise. I lifted the glass to thank my handsome benefactor. From the look of his suit, he was as rich as he was good looking.

Slowly, he made his way down and took a seat next to me. "She'll have another and so will I," he said to the bartender, his glass raised in the air.

"I'm Sam," he extended a hand to go along with the introduction.

"Celeste," I said, as I brought my hand to meet his.

Sam seemed to exude confidence without being too arrogant. I, on the other hand, was more arrogant than confident. Sam shared story after story, many about his family. His father, though a notable psychiatrist, had paled in comparison to his grandfather who had amassed the family fortune in diamond mines.

Our relationship took off that night, and soon blossomed into an enviable romance. It seemed fate had intervened once again and quite generously this time. The girl who was raised with hand me downs and crooked haircuts was now the object of a very wealthy man's attention. We shopped at Cartier for diamond earrings and Gucci for handbags. I simply admired something and it was mine. We dined in fine restaurants and drank imported champagne. Service was always immediate and impeccable. Sam was always treated preferentially, and as Sam's girlfriend, whether we were together or not, the same courtesies were extended to me.

Coincidentally, it turned out that we were both in the freight business, but we had different client bases. He catered mostly to the movie studios, while my business was devoted to the commercial customer looking to transport goods, both domestically and internationally.

Sam was impressed with my expertise and wanted me to come and work with him, but I'd just been promoted to director of sales and wasn't in the market for a new job. I also couldn't imagine giving up my independence, and working with Sam would have been doing just that. Still, no matter how many times I said no, Sam was relentless in his pursuit. He finally wore me down. We were going to conquer the movie industry together.

With our business interests now united, we worked even longer hours, through weekends, as well. Sam traveled back and forth between the California and New York offices, while I spent most of my time in New York. Our life together was good, even though together was more figurative than literal. It was getting harder and harder to find time for each other, so we agreed to take a break and get away, just the two of us. The next thing I knew, we were in Paris.

The Charles De Gaulle Hotel was the epitome of opulence. Hand embroidered draperies garnished floor to ceiling windows while filigree moldings framed walls and ceilings. The beauty was unnerving.

Our room was no different. From faucets to fixtures, the 19th century style of the Presidential Suite rendered me speechless. Surely, I had died and this was heaven. It took a few days to understand that my life had changed. This was now my new standard for living. The elegance was beyond dreams . . . beyond the imaginable. I wondered if anyone who hadn't experienced it could even comprehend such magnificence.

By the time I truly understood the meaning of lavish, we were on the Orient Express headed for Venice. The Hotel Danieli had been converted from separate castles dating back as early as the 14th century. With its elite clientele, having drinks with Bruce Stern and Robert Young was nothing out of the ordinary, nor was the display of original antiques, Murano glass chandeliers, or hand carved marble columns. By now, I'd expected nothing less.

When Sam suggested that we do some shopping while we were there, I was all for the idea.

Moreno glass, it turned out, was as pricey as it was beautiful. The black accent pieces would make a striking presentation when entertaining back home. So would the black place settings that were trimmed in gold. Any entrée would look like a culinary masterpiece served on that. And the coordinating glassware, also trimmed in gold, completed the dinner settings perfectly. We selected a few assorted trinkets for friends and family, and then headed to Valentino's where we were measured for custom gloves and shoes.

"This is the way you should always be treated," Sam insisted. I couldn't disagree.

Once the shopping was finished, we took a chartered a flight to the Southeast coast of France where a Rolls Royce awaited us. From there, we drove to La Bonne, a seaside spot in Cannes, where we toasted Dom Perignon and sampled caviar, then finished with an order of Chateaubriand for two. Five-hundred-and-fifty American dollars later, we were off to Monte Carlo for caviar and lobster at Du Paris. After trying our luck at the baccarat table, we settled into a fabulous suite for the night. The next morning, we went straight to Cartier before we flew back to Paris and went ballooning in Burgundy. Carried by a soft breeze over villages and vineyards, we finished off another perfect day.

After the whirlwind of activity over the last few days, we spent the next two strolling around town, dining on local fare, and pampering ourselves with every spa treatment available.

Taking time off together was wonderful, but it was back to real life the minute we touched down at Kennedy Airport. Sam was off to California the very next day and I was at my desk as soon as the sun had come up.

Even though our trip was like a fairy tale, Sam and I thrived on our everyday life. Business was everything to us, and we were happy to be devoted to it. Holidays even came second to business.

I can remember attempting dinners with my family, but they'd been annoyed that Sam had spent most of the time on the phone. He was always negotiating deals or resolving problems. They saw it as rude, but I found it appealing. Sam was an exceptional and highly skilled businessman. As long as he continued to treat me as well as he had, I didn't have a problem with it. In truth, if he hadn't been the one on the phone all those times, it would've been me.

CHAPTER TWENTY-ONE

White wicker seating and oversized floral arrangements were set between two huge pillars of the plantation style home. It was hard to believe this was New Jersey and not somewhere in the Deep South. Sam's description didn't do the Montvale estate justice, nor did it capture the breathtaking acreage with its lush gardens and flowing fountains.

Tippy was out front, waving madly. It didn't take long to see why Sam adored his mother. She was sweet and unpretentious, exactly as he'd described. And we became immediate friends. Tippy warned her son, "You'd better not let this one get away or you'll have me to deal with."

"Clearly, you've won my mother's heart." Sam's alluring smile was one of confidence. "All in good time," he said to his mother, though his eyes were fixed on me.

"No time like the present," she nudged.

He gave her a gentle kiss on the cheek. "It seems I don't have much of a choice, do I?"

I wasn't sure how I felt about that statement, so I quickly added with a grin, "There are always choices, Sam. It's just that some are not as wise as others."

"Let's go for a walk. It's a beautiful day," he suggested. I placed my hand in his and we set out along a path of blue stone and yellow perennials. Once we were a safe distance from the house, Sam turned to me and said, "Celeste, we're good together, like Bonnie and Clyde."

He asked if I got the picture. I chuckled slightly. "Not completely, but I think there's a message in there somewhere."

"You're beautiful, Celeste, and I love you. I could never imagine you with anyone else, only me. So . . . what do you say?"

"What do I say about what?" He laughed softly, and wrapped his arms around me. "I know I'll never meet anyone like you. I don't want to pressure you, but we need to plan our future."

As amazing and seemingly perfect our relationship was, I still wasn't ready for anything to change. Something wasn't quite right. Until I figured out what it was, I couldn't promise him more.

"Sam, I love you, too. But I think we should keep things as they are for right now. I'm just not ready for marriage."

We stayed overnight and the next day Tippy and I set out for the city. We shopped at Gucci, Versace, and then had a private showing at Saks. After that, it was Cartier, and then a late lunch at the Plaza. It was a lifestyle that I'd grown accustomed to and enjoyed immensely, but I just couldn't bring myself to plan a future with Sam, not just yet.

On the drive back to New Jersey, Tippy and I discussed the display of engagement rings we'd seen at Cartier. She'd insisted we take a look, just to see what they had. There was a five carat marquis stone in an antique setting that had captured my attention. "That's going to be your ring," she'd declared. "It suits you."

There couldn't be a more perfect mother-in-law, but I just wasn't ready to get married. Money wasn't the issue. Sam was more than generous, but my own investments had become very lucrative. My latest purchase, a commercial building, was now worth half-a-million dollars, and I was just about to purchase another one. There was also a waterfront condominium I'd been thinking about buying. It was a good feeling to be able to afford a lifestyle I could enjoy. I didn't have to rely on anyone and I didn't need permission for anything. There were even times when I said no to Sam, that I'd prefer to pay for things myself. I enjoyed having my own money to spend. Still, Sam wasn't able to accept that and insisted on paying for everything, even a phone for my Porsche. What should have been a kind and generous offer wasn't because he wasn't allowing for what I needed.

Besides that, I knew that there was still something that just wasn't right and I couldn't let it go.

Classical music played from hidden speakers and soft lighting emanated from wall sconces, as we flew to Chicago for dinner on Sam's private jet. The cabin was tastefully decorated with leather chairs, teak floors and a Flokati rug. We toasted Cristal champagne, nibbled on imported caviar, and fed each other fresh strawberries. Sam liked to use his own plane for domestic flights; that way there were no time constraints, but he did prefer to use the commercial carriers for overseas trips.

For my birthday we planned a wonderful day together starting with a champagne toast. We had an intimate lunch, just the two of us at the Plaza. Sam kissed my hand, his lips lingering before he let it go and slipped a black velvet box from his jacket pocket. Tears of joy trickled down my cheeks as I caressed the exquisite diamond necklace.

"Celeste, you've given my life purpose. I want to spend the rest of it with you." My mouth opened in surprise as Sam dropped onto one knee. "Marry me."

It was a necklace, not a ring. He caught me with the element of surprise. The entire restaurant watched as he offered his heart to me. And then, he stood and announced, "I just proposed to this wonderful woman." Applause rang out. "Wait," he said. "She hasn't said yes." He turned back to me and anxiously awaited his answer.

"Yes!" I shouted, a great big smile spreading across my face.

We toasted to our wedding and the life we would have.

"We'll be married here at the Plaza. And tomorrow we'll go to Tiffany's to pick out the ring," he said.

It seemed odd that he had chosen Tiffany's over Cartier. I assumed Tippy would have handled that with him.

He called his parents with the exciting news of our engagement and his plan to take me for a ring. Tippy demanded he take me straight to Cartier instead of Tiffany's.

And I'd actually doubted her!

CHAPTER TWENTY-TWO

The following evening we met Sam's parents at the Park Lane South Hotel. Owned by Harry Hemsley and given to his wife as a wedding present on their wedding day, it was the perfect choice for celebrating our engagement.

Tippy's delightful presence was a balance of grace, charm, and genuine warmth. Not to mention, she looked exquisite in her navy suit. Sam's father ordered the wine, imported of course, but more expensive than I'd ever seen. It was a style of living that never ceased to impress me. The evening was delightful and the conversation engaging. At some point, the discussion turned to wedding plans and where we would live. We agreed on two points that night; we would not live in New Jersey, and Tippy would handle all the arrangements for the wedding.

Between my upcoming business trips and trying to spend more time with Keith, there wasn't room for much else. Sam had scheduled a trip to Los Angeles and was leaving in a couple of days. So Tippy's offer was accepted with gratitude and relief.

While Sam was away I found myself busier than I'd planned. Sandy, one of our employees from the New York office had asked me to join her for dinner. I was exhausted. It had been another long day and I had no desire to dine with her, but it was easy to see there was something on her mind. I thought about it and since she had a reputation for kicking up dirt, I decided it was more prudent to hear her out now then diffuse some situation later.

"I'm not late am I?" I asked. Sandy's back was to me and her head tipped over a drink. She turned, acting almost surprised to see me. "Were you expecting someone else?" I asked.

"No, don't be silly," she said.

"Do you want to get a table or would you prefer we stay here?" I asked.

"A table." She slid off the bar stool, picked up her drink, and headed to the back of the restaurant.

Sandy had something big on her mind, but it was clear from all the small talk that she was going to take the long way around. I listened as she rambled on for almost an hour. We ordered a couple of burgers and that moved things along, but the evening had run its course. I had given her all the time she was going to get from me. "If there's nothing else you have to say, I'm going home. It's been a long day and I'm tired."

"Please, wait. There is something." She fidgeted with the salt and pepper shakers, the napkins, and then her glass.

"Look, I've had enough. Just say it."

"It's Sam. He's having an affair." I should've been stunned, but instead I just laughed at the ridiculous accusation. Sandy continued. "It's someone he works with."

"Well, what's her name? Who is she?"

"His secretary, Mary." Her eyes darted away and she appeared almost uncomfortable. I wondered if it could be true.

Sandy went into further detail and once she did, everything fell into place. That gnawing feeling that wouldn't go away made sense now. How could I be so stupid? What a fool I was. Why would he do this now, after three years, when we're about to get married? Rage mounted inside of me. "Check please." I tossed down enough to cover the bill and made a hasty exit.

Once I was safely in my car the tears came. My hands shook. I punched the steering wheel over and over again, yelling "Stupid, stupid, stupid."

The rain pelted my windshield. Even with the wipers at full speed it was hard to see, but I needed to get home. Just a few blocks from my apartment, I noticed there was a car behind me that had been there for quite a while. Then, I saw the hat. It was the same hat I'd seen on the man who was sitting at the bar in the restaurant. Was he following me, I wondered. Just to be sure, I made a few extra turns, checking my mirror to see. Yes, he was still behind me, so I pulled into a gas station and phoned the police. Within minutes there were cars everywhere. One officer detained him for questioning while another escorted me home. What a night it had been. And it wasn't over yet.

Summoning all the courage I could muster, I called Sam in Los Angeles. At first, he tried to deny the whole thing, but quickly switched tactics and went into apology.

"Why would you do this to us? To me? Was it a big joke to you?" Questions flew like bullets and I didn't wait for answers. Nothing could justify his betrayal. "We're through. Sam. Done. Finished."

"Please, Celeste, don't hang up. Let me explain."

"There's nothing to explain." I hung up the phone and dropped my head onto the pillow. Then, I sobbed for every broken promise and all the wonderful plans that would never be.

CHAPTER TWENTY-THREE

The following morning I called to cancel my appointment with Christian. He was a business associate of ours, based in France, and he'd come to the states for some appointments. I was supposed to meet with him around noon.

"Are you all right?" he'd asked at the sound of my voice.

"Yes, fine. I'll be all right."

"What's wrong? You don't sound like yourself."

"Nothing, except my life's a gigantic mess and I don't know what to do anymore."

"Is it Sam?"

"He's been having an affair with his secretary. I just found out and ended it with him last night."

"Celeste, darling, you shouldn't be alone right now."

"Christian, I'm too exhausted to even think. I don't even have the energy to drive. I can barely move."

"I'll come to you."

Less than an hour later, Christian was waiting out front. We took a ride into the city and walked around, talking about the mess that was now my life. He was compassionate, but did say he had suspected. There'd been rumors.

"Am I the only naive one around?" I asked. "How is it I didn't see the signs?"

He stopped walking and turned to face me. "You didn't want to see them. Did you?"

I stared at Christian, shocked by his words.

"Celeste, this isn't your fault. Sam's the guilty one. He should be begging your forgiveness."

I started walking again. "I'll never forgive him, Christian. How could I? He's broken my heart and made a mockery of our love. I never want to see him again. Never"

In a deliberate attempt to distract me, Christian suggested we go shopping. He left his car parked and called a limo to follow us around the entire day, collecting our packages in between stores.

"You've spent a small fortune on me," I protested at the end of the day.

"Beautiful things for a beautiful lady," he responded gallantly.

After dinner at The Four Seasons, we found a charming night spot on Park and drank ourselves into euphoria. Then, we capped off the night with champagne and chocolate dipped strawberries in a suite at the Hemsley Palace.

Everything I'd ever heard about the French was true. Christian asked me to return with him to Paris at the end of the week. "Maybe, after I settle things here," I said.

We drove back in silent bliss, the nightmare of Sam's infidelity far from concern. The answering machine flickered as we walked through the door. He was flying home. I didn't bother listening to the other messages, the one having already tainted the day.

"Christian, let's get out of here." He was more than anxious to please me and took me out for drinks and a bite to eat. By the time we got back, Sam was waiting in front of the building.

"Talk to him," Christian said. "See what you can work out. I'll give you some time together."

"Absolutely not. You're not going anywhere; he is. This will only take a minute."

I walked up to Sam, my gut churning with anger.

"What's Christian doing here?" he asked.

"Do you really think that's any of your business? You've given up all your rights." "Celeste, please, we have to talk."

"Talk about what?"

"About us, about our future."

"We have no future. Good-bye, Sam." I turned to walk away, but he grabbed my arm.

"You don't understand. I have to explain."

"There's nothing to explain," I said, as I pulled my arm from his grip. "Sam, it's over and I'm over you. Now, get back in your car and drive away before I call the police and have you arrested. I told you on the phone, there's nothing to talk about and I meant it."

"Listen, just leave her alone," Christian defended. He was standing close enough to hear, just in case I needed him. "She's been through enough, Sam."

"This is none of your business, Christian. Do yourself a favor and stay out of it."

"He's with me now, Sam, so you'd better back off."

"Please, Celeste, just give me a chance to explain. I can clear this whole thing up."

"Let him speak and then you'll be done. I can wait," Christian said.

Sam and I took a walk down the block. He insisted it was a one night stand, a huge mistake, and that he loved only me. But she was pregnant now, and threatened that he'd never see the baby if he ended it. That was the only reason he continued to see her.

"You know what, you deserve each other." And that was the last thing I said before I walked over to Christian and climbed into his car. Sam yelled, "If you leave me I'll kill myself, Celeste."

"Go ahead," I shouted. "I don't really care."

CHAPTER TWENTY-FOUR

Rob and I did our best to keep Keith out of our battles, but no matter how we tried to protect him we couldn't shield him from the pain. I loved my little boy, but what did I know about parenting? How could I understand his sadness when his Mommy was busy with work and showed up an hour late?

I wondered if ignorance counted as a defense. My whole adult life had been in response to my childhood, every action a reaction to something from back then. Unfortunately, my darling Keith became a casualty of that.

Though my marriage failed, never once did I think that Keith would've been better off with me. I was not abdicating my role as his mother. On the contrary, as his mother I had to make a very real decision. It was the hardest decision I've ever had to make, but I gave Keith what no one ever gave me, a stable home where he would be surrounded by a loving family. I knew Keith's parents would be the center of that home, and the ones to provide most of his care. In their capable hands, my son would flourish.

Rob never had much to give, except the ability to show up. When taking attendance, he was always there. But he had never been much of a provider. He couldn't even afford to buy me out of our house. Eventually, I agreed to a smaller settlement with a stipulation that a trust fund would be established for Keith's future.

My love for my son was enormous, but it was the guilt over leaving that overrode my anger at Rob for his financial incompetence. So when their furnace broke in the dead of winter, since I had the means, I provided a new one.

Besides necessities, I wanted to share some fun with Keith. Our time was limited, so I tended to look for elaborate ways to spend it with him. My heart ached to see his eyes light with excitement and hear the squeal of joy in his voice. I'd missed so much of his every day life that creating grand scale moments were important to me. It wasn't easy, though. During his younger years, Keith wasn't easily persuaded to leave the comfort of his home and go off with Mom. But as he got older, his love for sports won out over any apprehension he might have had in the past.

We sat front row to see Hulk Hogan wrestle at Madison Square Garden, the Rangers race a puck across the ice, and the Islanders at the Coliseum. Those were grand and cherished moments for the both of us.

Keith was about seventeen when he finally asked the question I always feared.

"Why did you leave?"

Like walking barefoot through shards of glass, carefully, I began. "Your father and I wanted different things, Keith. We had different ideas for what we wanted out of life. What's important is that we both love you."

"Dad said you were young and immature. That you had high expectations and wanted more than anyone could be expected to give."

"Keith, I wanted the best for all of us. And when you want certain things you have to work for them. And you have to work hard. Your father didn't believe in working hard for anything. He didn't care that much, but I did."

"You're talking about material things."

"Is this your father talking, Keith?"

"I just think there are a lot more important things to work for than what you can buy with money."

"Some people have a dream. They have goals. My dream was to make us comfortable and give you the best that life has to offer. I grew up in foster care and no one gave me anything. That made me all the more determined to make sure you would have everything you needed and wanted. Can you understand that?"

"Mom that's just about material things. You traded me for material things."

"No, Keith. By working hard I provided for you, made sure you had a roof over your head and never went to bed hungry like I did. I made sure you had nice clothes, perfect haircuts, parties and presents, and plenty of toys. Keith, those were the things that I never had. Those are the things that every child deserves."

I couldn't tell Keith about what drove us apart, about the money his father wasted on alcohol and nonsense. If he knew about the debt, the lies, the manipulations, it would only hurt him. He thought of Rob as the stable one. I couldn't take that away from him. Instead, I attempted to teach Keith about self-esteem and a good work ethic, sheltering him from the truth about his father's laziness and lack of ambition, that without me he probably would have lived in a shed.

My father-in-law, too, still suffered from the sting of what had happened. One day, he just broke down and asked, "How could you have just left us?"

It was still difficult to talk about, as if it had happened yesterday. "Do you think it was my first choice to leave? You know how long I tried, but it was your son's abuse that chased me away." My defense continued. "I worked full time, and then came home to take care of the baby, make dinner, and straighten up. It was all without any help from Rob. He'd carry on in a drunken stupor the whole time, making it even harder for me. You know what I suffered. You know what a nasty drunk he was."

"How can you blame me?"

I sought understanding when I needed forgiveness. What I got was silence.

CHAPTER TWENTY-FIVE

As a child, all I ever wanted was to be loved and valued. Instead, I was abused, humiliated, and deprived. It could have broken me, but it didn't. I knew one day I'd have my chance, and then I would be responsible for myself, choosing who and what I allowed into my life. With a solid work ethic, I inched my way along and did very well. But that was business.

There was always one piece refusing to snap into place, motherhood. I just couldn't seem to get it right. Years of confrontations and remorse finally led me into counseling.

"I'd had just a hint of what a mother could be," I told the therapist. "I'd met my own mother only once before she died. She'd been hospitalized shortly after my birth. They said it was a nervous breakdown. She never recovered, but on one of her good days she did come to see me. I was about eight or nine at the time, home sick from school. Sal, my biological father, had planned to come, but I never expected him to bring my mother along.

I remember her dark red hair and beautiful, porcelain complexion. She didn't look sick at all. Her smile was tender and I can remember how she gently kissed my cheek. When she asked how I was feeling my father yelled at her to say something else. My mother saw how his voice agitated me, so she ran her fingers through strands of my hair to calm me down. There were tears in her eyes after that. She said I would get better. She said God would always be with me. That's when my father snapped at her. He said God had done nothing for him and asked why she said such stupid things.

It was our first and only visit, and he ruined it. I never saw her again, until her funeral later that year. I wanted her to know I was there, so I touched her hand. It was cold and hard, not like the day she came to my room. I hid in the coat room after that, crying. I hardly knew her, but I'd always dreamed that one day she'd come for me.

"That's understandable," the therapist responded.

"Even though I hardly knew her and we only had the one visit, I dreamed of being like her, gentle and kind, but then circumstances got in the way and I never had the opportunity to be the kind of mother I hoped to be. Sometimes Keith is like a stranger to me, someone I've just met. I know that's wrong. I'm supposed to feel more."

The therapist explained about my detachment, my inability to bond. "You've had no frame of reference. You couldn't possibly understand a mother's nurturing love without having experienced it, Celeste. But you do show Keith your love by providing for his financial needs, and also by making sure he has a stable and loving home environment. In that way, you're as dedicated as any mother could be."

Her explanation made perfect sense and settled that piece that had never snapped into place. The sessions gave me the awareness I needed in order to accept my limitations and release the guilt I'd been carrying. From that point on, I was content to be the best mother I possibly could, the one I had always been.

CHAPTER TWENTY-SIX

After several business trips to Ireland, I closed a deal on a little farm there. Someday, when the time was right, my plan was to retire there. In the meantime, some friends who had their own place just down the road were going to look in on the property for me.

I'd kept up with the commercial investments and was also working at the airport again. Selling freight services had always been a good fit for me. No matter the company, I always out performed everyone else and worked my way into a management position. It was a relatively calm time in my life, things were moving along nicely with hardly a hitch in anything business or personal.

That's when I met him. It was another drink at another bar and a different group of friends this time, but there he was, strikingly attractive and filthy rich. Jeff was a perfect candidate for a romance, even though he happened to have been engaged.

The Rainbow Room had always been a favorite of mine. The Duck Flambé and Cherries Jubilee were culinary masterpieces. Maybe that was why it had only taken Jeff a week to talk me into going.

It was a perfect evening, but as I took a last sip of champagne I knew being there with him was a mistake.

"Jeff, I've made enough mistakes in my life to know this can only take me someplace I don't want to go." I thanked him and wished him all the best. He told me to call if I changed my mind. Then, kissed my cheek and stood watching as I drove off.

The next day I was shocked to hear his voice on the other end of the line. "Jeff, I'm on my way into a meeting. Talk fast. Tell me why you called."

"There's something I'd like to discuss. Would you meet me for lunch?"

"I can't. This meeting could run into the afternoon."

"Okay, dinner then?"

"I can't say right now . . . my business is like that sometimes."

"Can I call you later?"

"Fine, later."

The meeting dragged on even longer than expected and my mind kept wandering to Jeff. What could he possibly have to discuss? It shouldn't have mattered anyway, but by the time the meeting was over I knew I'd be having dinner with him.

We met at the restaurant and exchanged pleasantries over a glass of wine before Jeff unleashed his big news. He couldn't go through with his planned marriage while he had such a deep interest in me, an interest he wanted to pursue. I agreed to spend some time with him, just to see if there was something worth pursuing.

The test was a success. We spent a fabulous weekend together. We had lunch in the city, and then drove to the East End of Long Island for dinner. As the moonlight reflected off the water, Jeff and I held hands and talked the night away. He gave me a mahogany music box. When I opened the lid, it played *Over the Rainbow*. I knew then that it was only the beginning for us.

We continued to see each other, sharing dreams of what a future together would hold, but it wasn't long before I was ready for more. I would no longer tolerate sharing him with another woman. That left Jeff with a big decision. He had to choose.

Weeks went by and true to my resolve I hardly spoke to Jeff. He'd called a few times, but I didn't always answer. I needed to keep my life moving forward without him, unless he was willing to break off his engagement.

After an extended business trip to Europe and a few days of relaxation in Ireland, it was time to settle my feelings for Jeff. I'd kept him at a safe distance, but that didn't do much for my thoughts. Jeff had become an unwelcome distraction, and I had far more important issues that warranted my attention.

It couldn't have been more than a few minutes that I'd been back. Just as I'd tossed my luggage on the bed, the door bell rang. I tiptoed across the living room and looked through the peephole. There was Jeff, standing at my door. I waited quietly hoping he would leave. As exhausted as I felt, there was no way I was ready to have any kind of serious discussion. When he left, I went back into the bedroom and unpacked, and then I took a nice long nap. Other than getting up for a quick snack, I slept the entire afternoon and night. Sunday morning, I woke with the sun filtering through the blinds.

There were five messages on the answering machine. They were all from Jeff. I was in no hurry to speak to him, so I took a shower and got dressed before returning his call.

"Where are you?" The alarmed tone was hard to miss.

"And hello to you, too."

"Are you all right?" he asked.

"Of course I am. How are you?"

"I'm fine, but I was worried. Where'd you go? And more importantly, why didn't you tell me you were leaving?"

"Was I supposed to check in with you? I wasn't aware of that."

"Celeste, we have to talk."

"Talk about what?"

"Us."

"Which us would that be?"

"Celeste, please. Give me a chance to say what I need to."

"I'm pretty booked right now. I just got back last night, so I'll have to check my planner and get back to you."

"Why don't we just meet for dinner tonight?"

"No, I'm still tired from all the traveling. Let me call you later."

After some thought, I decided it was better to get this over with than drag it out, so I pulled out my date book and called Jeff back.

We met at a restaurant on Tuesday. It was time to finish this up.

"Celeste," Jeff took my hands in his. "You are all I can think about. It's been impossible to focus on anything else. I've decided to break it off with Brooke."

That was the last thing I'd expected to hear and I didn't know how to respond. I was speechless and sat there searching his eyes for signs of truth.

"Are you going to tell me how you feel about my decision?"

"I'm not exactly sure what to say. Perhaps you'd like to share your reasons for such a life changing decision."

"Obviously, you haven't been listening to a word I said or you wouldn't ask such a question."

"I heard what you said, but I'm not sure I believe that you're ready to do what you said."

He looked straight at me. His jaw was as rigid as stone. "Just promise me you'll give me the chance to show you I'm serious. Please."

Even though I still had doubts, we agreed to move forward, as soon as he met with Brook and took care of what had to be done. Brooke was not about to give up without a fight; I knew that much. Since his livelihood was tied to her family, she did have the advantage.

"Until things are settled, Jeff, I'd prefer it if we didn't talk. Please respect my feelings." I tilted my head upward and placed a hand on each of his cheeks. "I'll always care about you, regardless of what happens this weekend." Then, I kissed him and walked off.

Jeff called and left a message later that evening. "I'll do the right thing for us. I promise."

Even though it was early, I tried to fall sleep. Anything that would keep me from thinking about Jeff was a good thing. But instead of sleeping I tossed and turned as the voice of my foster father tormented me. No matter how much I had accomplished, I could still hear him telling me I was no good for anything, ugly and stupid, and not worth the money the state put out for me.

When the phone rang, I jumped. It was Maria. Although she disliked Jeff, she knew this weekend would be hard for me and called to invite me out for a drink.

NEVER SAY NEVER

"Maybe later, I'll call you in a while," I promised.

Maria's heart was as big as the ocean. She was a brilliant and dedicated pediatric intern at Mt Sinai Hospital in Manhattan. Her only fault was that she had a tendency to embellish. She'd hear about someone with a broken finger and by the time Maria was through telling the story, it was an amputation, at least. Still, it was easy to forgive her for her creativity because nothing was ever intended for harm. For Maria, that would have been impossible.

Every year at Christmas time, Maria would take me to the pediatric floor of the hospital where we'd hand out gifts to the children. Her love permeated that ward like nothing I'd ever seen before. Maria was a natural giver, always filling everyone with hope.

As for me, she'd often tease how I'd climb over anyone to get what I want. Yet, that was exactly the trait she admired most.

"Take no prisoners," I'd always respond. And then we'd laugh.

She often encouraged me to rise above my circumstances and see things from her viewpoint. It worked just as well that way because her viewpoint was always slanted in my favor anyway.

Though Maria was a source of inspiration and support for me, I still couldn't bring myself to leave the cocoon-like environment of my apartment.

"I'm sorry, Sweetie; I'm going to have to pass. I just don't have it in me tonight." I hung up the phone and curled back up on the couch.

Monday came and I still hadn't heard from Jeff. Maria had called it right when she said he wouldn't have the balls to leave Brooke. She insisted I deserved better than him. I came home from work to find a message from Jeff, waiting on my machine. "Sorry it took so long," he said. "There's a lot to talk about. Meet me at Justin's about seven, but don't leave your apartment until I call that I'm on my way."

I took a shower and threw on a pair of jeans, fixed my make-up and hair, and still there was no call. It was an odd request to begin with and by now I was convinced Jeff was a no show. At ten the phone rang. I nearly broke my leg jumping over the coffee table to reach it in time.

"Did he call?" Maria asked.

"Yes and no." I went on to explain the mysterious plan and the follow up call that never came.

Maria came right back with her response. "Bastard! Dump his sorry ass."

The next morning, on my way to work, Jeff called my cell to apologize. He explained there were extenuating circumstances and insisted we needed to talk. I told him he had his chance and he missed it.

"Brooke's ill," he blurted out.

"And?"

"I can't leave her now. Not like that. I'm so sorry. Will you meet me? I'll explain more when I see you."

"Jeff, I don't need you to explain anything more. You were a big waste of my time and I'm not going to give you one more minute of it."

I wanted to snap the phone in half, but settled for turning it off. Then with a shove, I stuffed it all the way down in my bag, instead of tossing it into a nearby garbage can. I'd already lost enough to Jeff.

It wasn't a surprise that this happened. I'd tried to prepare myself, yet my heart was still broken. I turned around and went home, and called in sick. Then, I threw a few things into a bag and headed for Montauk. Gurney's Inn had one room left. I took it.

I walked the beach for two days wondering why they always look so good, and then they go bust. Why had I believed him anyway? Maybe I didn't. Maybe I just hoped that this time would be different, but it wasn't. Different time, different place, same old disappointment. All that mattered was that it was time to move forward.

As I checked out and headed for my car, my cell rang.

"Celeste, please. I need to explain."

"Jeff, leave me alone. There's nothing you can say that I would believe. I don't want to hear another word out of those lying lips. Understand?" I hung up and got into my car and headed home, tears

NEVER SAY NEVER

streaming down my cheeks.

Everyone would soon find out that Jeff and I were through. They probably didn't expect it to last anyway. In all honesty, I didn't either.

CHAPTER TWENTY-SEVEN

Jeff had been just another disappointment added to the list. It took me about a week to recover, but as soon as I had, I called Maria to see if she was free for dinner.

"Are you in the mood for Italian tonight?"

"Sorry, Celeste, but this week's absolutely insane. I am glad, however, that you're finally over that loser. How about if we go out next Wednesday to celebrate?"

"You're on!"

The week had passed without a word from Maria and by the time Wednesday had come around I thought it was odd that she hadn't even called to confirm. It was her first day off in two weeks, so I assumed she'd been caught up in a flurry of activity and just left a quick reminder on her cell.

If it had been anyone else, I would have gotten up and walked out after my second drink. But Maria was like a sister to me and she would never stand me up. It must've been important if she was a no show. Kenny, the bartender, who was also a close friend of Maria's hadn't seen or heard from her either. I'll call one more time, I told him.

"Maria, where are you? I'm getting bombed waiting for you."

Maria had been upset about her father. He'd been diagnosed with stomach cancer and was undergoing radiation treatments. Maybe something happened with him.

"Do me a favor," I finally said to Kenny, "if she ever shows up or calls, tell her to call me. I'm going home.

As I rode up in the elevator, I couldn't help but worry that something was seriously wrong. Two men in suits were standing by my door. I knew it wasn't good news they were bringing. I swallowed hard and walked toward them.

"Are you Celeste?" the taller of the two asked.

"Yes, I am. Who are you?" They showed me badges. They were detectives from the local precinct.

"Can we come in?"

"Why? What's this about?"

"I think it's better if we talk inside," the other one said.

We took seats on the couch. "I'm sorry to tell you this, but there's been an accident. Your friend, Maria, is in the hospital."

"Hospital? What happened?" I slid forward, ready to go. "Her car was hit head on. She's in a coma."

I stood, tears trickling, my mind not quite grasping anything other than the thought that I had to get to her.

The officers stood. "The doctors are working on her right now. Her family's already there. Maybe it'd be better if you waited a little while, calm down a little before you drive. The last thing your friend needs now is for you to get into an accident. Maybe if you waited until morning and let the news settle in you'll be able to think a little clearer, function a little better.

They were very kind and I promised I would wait, but the minute they left I was dialing Maria's mother. Voice mail! "It's Celeste. I heard what happened. Please call me . . . day or night. I'm here for you."

Next, I dialed Maria's brother and his voice mail came on, too. "It's Celeste. The police just left. They told me what happened. I was supposed to meet her tonight. Please call me."

About twenty minutes later the phone rang. It was Joe, Maria's brother. He was crying so hard I could hardly make out a word he was saying.

"Calm down, so I can understand you."

"Maria's in a coma."

"Yes, I heard . . . The police were here. I'd just gotten back. She was supposed to meet me. She never showed. Joe, I was so worried. I knew something was wrong. Maria would never stand me up without calling."

"It doesn't look good. The doctors don't think . . ." Joe's words trailed off, replaced by loud sobbing.

I wanted to scream and cry right along with Joe, but I had to stay calm. I'd be of no use to anyone if I fell apart now.

"Sit down. Breathe. Just breathe, honey. Do you want me to come?" I waited a minute while he quieted himself before he could answer.

"No, it would be better if you waited until morning. There's nothing you can do right now. Nothing any of us can do, except wait."

We left off with his promise to call again in a few hours. Immediately I dialed Donna, a friend who worked in the emergency room where Maria had been taken, hoping she would tell me something more.

"All I've heard is that it was a bad blow to the head. She's in a coma. From what they said, there's very little brain activity. They're still running tests. I can keep you posted if you like, but I doubt there'll be any news before morning."

"Thank you, but I'll be there in the morning."

Thirty minutes later, Maria's mother called. "I spoke to Maria today and she told me she was going to meet you for dinner."

"Yes, and when she didn't show I was worried. You know that's not like Maria. She would have called."

"Celeste, how are you holding up? Are you okay?"

Her daughter was lying in a hospital bed and this wonderful woman was asking about me.

"I'm fine, just worried about Maria and all of you. Tell me, what I can do to help? Just say the word, anything at all."

"Nothing, darling. You've been such a good friend to my Maria. But there's nothing any of us can do right now. Get some rest and you can come see her in the morning. We've been taking turns talking to her. You can have a turn tomorrow."

"I'll be there. If anything changes before then, anything at all, please call me."

"Of course, dear. And I wanted to let you know, Maria's father doesn't know about any of this. He was admitted to the hospital last week and we've decided not to upset him with the news, for now. There's nothing he can do anyway. And in his condition, well, he's just not strong enough."

"I understand. You're right, of course."

It was one o'clock in the morning and sleep was far from coming, so I called Kenny to tell him the news.

"Celeste, I knew it was you. I had a feeling. What's going on?"

He was in shock when I told him and wanted to know if there was anything he could do. "Pray," I replied. "That's all anyone can do." With that, I broke down. My body shook as tears streamed; it all poured out, right into Kenny's ear.

He did his best to console me, insisting we had to have faith. "We just have to believe, Celeste. God will do the rest."

The rest of the night, I tossed and turned and hardly got a wink of sleep. By seven in the morning, I was dressed and ready to go to the hospital.

CHAPTER TWENTY-EIGHT

The lobby was quiet when I arrived at the information desk, giving Maria's name to the volunteer.

"I'm sorry, it's family only. Are you family?" the gray haired woman asked.

Joe's voice came from behind me. "Yes, she is."

"Thank you," I said to the woman, as she handed me a visitor's pass.

Joe took my arm, led me to the elevator, and we shared a teary embrace.

Maria's mother seemed relieved that I'd come. She gave me a big hug, and then told me to go and talk to Maria.

"Has anything changed?" I asked.

"Not yet, but they're still testing."

I just nodded, then pushed the oversized door open and stepped inside, clicking it closed behind me. Tubes, wires, and machines were everywhere. Monitors beeped away, recording heart, breathing, and brain activity. As I bent down and kissed her cheek, I knew that these machines were the only thing keeping her alive. And then I prayed for strength.

"Maria," I chided. "This is no way to get me to see you on a weekday. You could have simply insisted." Then, I launched into a monologue on how inconvenient it was to be stood up. "I mean, all you had to do was cancel." I babbled on, confident she was listening to every word.

It was so hard to see her this way. I swallowed the lump forming in my throat. "You have to wake up," my voice cracked. "Yell at me. Tell me I have too much make-up on, something, anything, just please wake up."

With the back of my hand I swiped at the wetness on my cheeks. I took a deep breath, and then leaned over to whisper in her ear. "Unless you get up soon, I'm going to crawl into that bed with you. People will talk. I'm telling you, they will."

Tears fell faster, as I watched the ventilator force air in and out of her lifeless body. "Look what you're doing to me. Pretty soon there'll be so much water we'll need a boat to get us out of here." I gave a soft, almost exasperated chuckle, mopping my face with a tissue I'd pulled from my bag.

I wanted to get mad. Didn't she know how much I needed her? We shared everything: good times, disappointments, conflicts too, but she never gave up on us. She loved me, faults and all.

"Hey, Maria, do you remember Club Med?" I asked. "You had your eye on that pastry chef. Every night he would send us the most delicious and fattening pastries. I must have gained ten pounds on that trip, just so you could flirt with the guy. Now that's friendship!"

For over an hour I sat there talking to her, willing her to wake up. I would have continued, too, if her sister hadn't come in.

Nancy hugged me. "I'm so glad you're here. She paused, biting down on her lip. "You've been such a good friend to Maria." Her nostrils flared as she sucked in a breath, trying to hold back tears.

"Maria's been like a sister to me." I swallowed hard. "I'll give you some time alone with her," I offered, before my own tears fell again.

With my head down, I walked into the hallway and leaned against the wall. I closed my eyes and sucked in a great big breath. Then, pursed my lips and slowly released the air.

Nancy didn't stay long. Only minutes had passed before the door opened.

"I could use a cup of coffee," she said to me. "A strong one."

I nodded. I understood.

"Would you like to join me?" she asked.

"Sure, I could use one, too."

NEVER SAY NEVER

We took the elevator to the main floor and found the coffee shop in the back of the building.

"Nancy, I know this is hard for you to talk about and I'm sorry to ask, but I don't understand how this happened." I needed information, something that would make sense. All I had were pieces and nothing seemed to fit.

"Some guy went barreling through a light," she said. "He hit her head on. The car flipped over, ramming her head against the driver's side window and causing the coma.

The doctors say her chances for recovery aren't good. There's been no brain activity. A specialist is coming in later today to consult with the team here. We'll know more then."

I took a sip of the steamy black liquid, and then wrapped my hands around the cup.

"We thought it was best not to tell my father. I'm sure Maria told you he has cancer."

I just nodded.

"He's in a hospital across town and we didn't want to upset him until we know more."

"Yes, your mother mentioned that."

"And I'm concerned about her, too. She has to run back and forth between the two of them now. It's a lot for her, physically as well as emotionally."

"Certainly you can count on me to help with anything you need. I hope you know that."

"I was hoping to go with my mother to visit my father, later today. So if you could stay here with Joe that would take some of the burden off."

"Of course, I'll be here as long as you need me, probably longer." We dropped empty cups into the waste basket and went back to Maria's room, taking turns sitting with her.

After Nancy and her mother had gone, Joe and I alternated shifts talking to Maria, willing her back to life.

"Are you awake? I could sure use a glass of wine, but there'll be none for you, miss." I chuckled lightly. "Okay, fine, I'll wait until you can have some, too."

For hours, I sat there and watched as doctors, nurses, and technicians floated through the room to check equipment, monitor vitals, and take endless blood samples; all of them looking for signs of improvement. In between rotations with Joe, I called my office and arranged to take some vacation time.

Maria's mother called and let me know she was going home to change and get a little rest before coming back. The doctors had given her the grim news, her husband wasn't doing well. The only thing left was to keep him comfortable.

I waited until she returned, and then went home to shower and sleep. The next day, I stopped off to visit Maria's father. I gave him a hug and we talked for a while, but I was careful to avoid any topic having to do with Maria.

The rest of the week I spent mostly by Maria's bedside, the nurses smiling warmly at me as they tended to their duties, checking equipment and jotting notes. It was after nine long days when Maria's mother was given the prognosis. She called me into the hall to tell me.

"There's been no change; still no sign of brain activity. The doctors say Maria will never regain consciousness."

I took her hands in mine as tears trickled from her red, swollen eyes.

"They say there's nothing more they can do. We have to have her transferred to a care facility, unless we decide to take her off support."

I swallowed hard. No, Maria was going to get better. She had to. There were so many horrible people in the world. Why couldn't it be one of them?

I took a deep breath and let out a long sigh, then nodded in understanding before retreating back to Maria's room. Squeezing carefully onto the edge of the bed, I took her hand in mine. How could I say good-bye? She'd helped me through so much pain in my life, how would I get through this without her? As if she could hear me . . . *You can do this, Celeste. You're strong enough.* Her voice came to me, as clearly as if she'd spoken it out loud.

Joe and Nancy were locked in a tight embrace when I emerged from the room.

"We're taking her off support," their mother had said. "She wouldn't want us to leave her like that." With a handful of scrunched up tissues, she dabbed at moist eyes.

"When?" I asked.

"Tonight," she said, barely above a whisper.

I nodded.

She put a hand to her chest and cleared her throat before continuing. "They don't think she'll survive the night, not without the ventilator. But if she does, they'll transfer her to another facility in the morning. For whatever time is left."

We all shared a teary embrace. Just breathe, I told myself, as I stepped back, tears trickling down my cheeks. I swiped at them, quickly, and then excused myself to find the chapel.

It was a dimly lit room, carpeted in blue, with rows of upholstered chairs arranged in front of a small altar. I took a seat in the back and dropped my head into my hands. Maria was going to leave me, my heart cried out in pain. "Help me to understand." I looked up at the altar as if God were standing there Himself. "She's so good, helps so many . . . Why?" My voice crackled. "I've prayed, begged, and pleaded. I just don't understand." As I sobbed, my head fell back to my hands

"Are you okay?" Startled and embarrassed, I turned at the sound of Joe's voice. I hadn't heard him come in. He walked over and sat beside me, then held me close while I cried. "What kind of God allows something like this to happen?" I asked. Joe didn't answer, just sat quietly as he brushed away tears with his sleeve. I dropped my head onto his shoulder and whispered, "How will you tell your father?"

"I don't know," he answered, then sighed deeply.

CELESTE ROTH

The door creaked open and a shaft of light from the hall rushed in. "It's your father; he's in a coma," the voice softly declared. "We have to go, now." Joe stood obediently and rushed to his mother's side, the door closing behind them with a click.

I looked at the oversized cross on the wall and wondered how one family was supposed to deal with all of this.

While they were gone, I sat with Maria, holding her hand. At eleven, the staff came in to check her vitals, and then, if nothing had changed the plan was to disconnect the life support. But that was before the family had been called away. Because of the extenuating circumstances, the hospital agreed to postpone.

The phone rang shortly before midnight. "Dad's not doing well. It looks as though he'll be leaving us first," Nancy said, her voice unnaturally calm as though reporting a news event.

The next morning, when she walked in with swollen eyes, I knew.

"I'm so sorry, Nancy." I held her while she spilled fresh tears. How would she find the strength to bury both her father and sister?

Two of Nancy's friends had come to sit with Maria while the rest of us showered and tended to funeral arrangements. The hospital had agreed to wait until after the burial, which gave us some time to invite Maria's co-workers to say farewell.

Maria's mother pulled me aside. "You've been a wonderful friend to this family," she said, and then gave me a big hug before getting to the details of the arrangements. "The wake will be tomorrow, honey, the burial the following day. After that, we'll talk about the life support."

It was decided that Maria's support would be disconnected on the following Monday. The weeks of agony were almost over, but in another way just beginning.

When the day came, Nancy, Joe, Maria's mother, and I all took turns saying good-bye. Afterward, Joe and I went for a walk. By the time we got back, the support had been disconnected and Maria was breathing on her own.

The four of us stayed through the night and it was around seven

NEVER SAY NEVER

in the morning when I decided to get a cup of coffee. That's when I felt the strange sensation. I took her hand in mine and assured her I'd be right back; I was only going to get coffee.

By the time I came back, Maria had passed.

CHAPTER TWENTY-NINE

The pain of losing Maria was so deep that I stumbled through the next year, barely able to think of anything other than what would become of me now that she was gone. It was the year of the great depression, and took longer than that before I was finally able to visit her.

The stone marker told very little about the woman resting there, only that she died too young. It didn't speak of the person I'd known, the reason I missed her so much.

"I know it's been a while, but I'm here now," I told my dear friend. "I just couldn't do it any sooner. But you'll forgive me, just like you always have." I smiled and a tiny laugh escaped, as I thought of what Maria would have said to that.

"So I'm sure you want to know what's been happening. For starters, I met a doctor. But that didn't work out. Then, I met a lawyer, but that didn't work out either. There was that nuclear physicist, but I almost had to have him arrested. He all but attacked me when he walked me to my car one night. I'm sure you'll agree that I'm dating a much better class of losers these days.

It's been a tough road for me without you, and I'm going to be honest; I've put on a lot of weight. Still, you can't get mad at me because it's your fault." I cleared some of the weeds away, settling them into a small pile. "I'll take the weight off, eventually. I always do.

I've been trying to spend more time with Keith. I know you think that's a good idea. You wouldn't believe how he's growing! Oh, and did I tell you, out of sheer boredom I joined the volunteer fire department; the one in Bethpage. That's where I live now. With you gone, I couldn't stay in Long Beach anymore . . . passing your door everyday. I even sold my real estate holdings around there. It was just too hard to go back. And that property in Ireland, I sold that, too. I've given up on dreaming.

Would you believe I was a millionaire? I was, until I blew through it all. Without you around dispensing your wisdom, I became a pauper. I had to take a job with a pharmaceutical company. The pay stinks, but I was desperate. At night, I'm working in a gym as a personal trainer, just to make the bills. Would you believe I count pennies to do the wash? Talk about depressing!

Well, it's time for me to get going, but I'll be back to see you again. I promise."

It was strangely comforting, rambling on about everything she'd missed. Maybe next time I'd bring some wine for us. I smiled at the idea.

Leaving the cemetery I thought about the jobs I had applied for, at least fifty of them. Every single interview was the same; they all said I was overqualified. The once confident and successful Celeste had somehow lost her touch.

It took a while, but things eventually turned around, as they always did. After losing the excess weight I was able to get a job at a much better gym, one that attracted a better clientele. It was there that I met a group of investors who invited me to join their circle of friends. Impressed with my background, one even offered me a share of his real estate deal; a strip mall with twelve stores, all occupied and doing well. And he had no problem structuring the agreement without any cash up front.

Opportunities like that rarely came around and I wasn't about to pass it up. Once the deal was in place, my confidence returned and I was certain I'd soon be able to repay the benevolence, with interest. And that was exactly how it happened, which opened the door to a second deal.

Together, my partner and I purchased another successful market place, but six months later he announced that he was getting out. His eye was on a business in Los Angeles and he made me an incredible offer to buy him out. I'd already managed to pay back most of the seed money and had tucked a little something away as well, so I jumped at the deal.

My former success had been restored and I was happy to be on my own again, but eventually, the market started to turn and I liquidated my holdings. Unsure of what I wanted to do, I began to reconstruct the life I'd once enjoyed: traveling, fine dining, expensive wardrobes, and the finest jewelry. Everything I wanted was once again mine, until the money ran out.

CHAPTER THIRTY

I was undaunted by the fact that I was broke again. Money would find me again. It always had. In the meantime, other than an occasional dinner out with the girls, I was content to stretch out on the couch with a pint of Haagen Dazs in one hand and a large spoon in the other, watching *America's Most Wanted*.

One Saturday night, my bliss had been interrupted by my friend, Susan. She'd called to invite me to join her and her boyfriend, Andrew. "Enough of this recluse thing, we're going to a club and you're coming with us; we're not taking no for an answer. Your only choice is if you want to drive yourself or if you want us to pick you up?"

"I'm just not in the mood, really. I appreciate your concern, but I'm fine right where I am."

"That wasn't one of the choices. We'll pick you up at ten-thirty."

"Ten-thirty? I'll be in bed by then."

"Not tonight you won't."

"I'll meet you there," I said, even though I wasn't happy about it.

"Over here." Susan's arm was waved wildly the minute she saw me walk in. "Here, sit down," she patted the chair next to her. "Order something."

"Scotch rocks, neat," I said to the waiter. When I finished my drink, I ordered another, and then another. After three drinks, I finally started to loosen up enough to laugh at Susan's ridiculous stories.

The next weekend, Susan and Andrew were on my doorstep, uninvited. "Did you eat yet? We're taking you to dinner."

"Susan, stop," I argued. "Three's a crowd," I protested, my hand up, palm facing her.

"Fine, we'll stay here and order in. You can pay."

"Never mind," I squeezed my lips, shaking my head from one side to the other. "I'll take a shower and be ready in fifteen minutes. Okay?"

After a large portion of lasagna and a generous piece of cheesecake, we headed over to the club again.

"Just one drink," Susan promised, but one drink turned into two, and then into three. Finally, Andrew went to pay the bill as Susan and I headed for the door.

"Excuse me," I said, as I bumped into a really good-looking guy who was just walking in, my neck craning for a second look. Susan noticed him, too.

"C'mon," she said. "You're going to meet him."

"Are you kidding?" I asked, exasperated. Apparently she wasn't kidding. She was already closing in on him, seconds from active conversation. I looked on in disbelief, shaking my head from side-to-side. Her finger stretched in my direction and the next thing I knew he was making his way through the crowd, heading straight for me.

"Hi, I'm Stephen."

"I'm so embarrassed. I have to apologize for my friend. She's incorrigible."

"Don't be silly. I'm glad she gave me the opportunity to meet you. I was afraid you were leaving and I wouldn't get the chance."

"Well, in that case I guess I'll have to forgive her for her impulsiveness." My mouth curled into a soft smile.

"Would you like to sit down? It looks like there are a couple of spots open over there on the couch." One of his hands was on the small of my back, the other pointed out the direction.

"Sure," I smiled, my skin shivering at his touch.

We talked for a few minutes, but only briefly because Susan and Andrew were waiting.

"I'm sorry, but I do have to go," I told him. "We were actually on our way out just as you came in." His eyes followed mine as I glanced to Susan and Andrew who were waiting by the door. "They're my ride."

"Can I call you? Later, perhaps?"

My mind raced with possibilities and I wasn't sure if I was ready to for another let down, but in spite of my reservations we exchanged phone numbers and agreed to talk later.

It was after two in the morning when I walked into my apartment, certainly too late for anyone to call. But just as I climbed under the cover, the phone rang.

"Guess who?" came the voice on the other end.

I smiled.

"I know it's late, but I can't stop thinking about you. Can I see you again? Don't answer now; I'll call you in the morning," Stephen said.

The phone rang at eight o'clock. Two hours later we were still talking and by one we were strolling around town enjoying a lovely, sunny day. He took me by surprise, pulling me into a burly embrace, my body just about melting as his lips lowered to mine. It was the perfect, fairy-tale kind of kiss; I could even picture the pixie dust swirling around.

"I'm going to marry you one day," he declared with boldness.

I just nodded, dreamy-eyed and smiling.

Later that day, after he'd gone, I decided he was simply too good to be true. Based on my previous history with men, what were the odds that he was *the one*? I convinced myself that it was nothing more than a wonderful day and accepted the likelihood that he wouldn't call again.

Once that was settled it was easier to move on with my day. I confirmed dinner plans with a friend, ran a few errands, and then went home to get ready. When I walked in the light on the answering machine was flashing.

"Call me. I miss you."

My eyebrows furrowed; was this guy for real?

I called him back and he picked up on the first ring. "I missed you," he said.

"Do you know who this is?" I asked.

We talked for about an hour and made plans to meet at a little Italian place on Monday.

Then, pressed for time, I raced to get ready for dinner.

The evening turned out nice, but I was tired from the day and couldn't wait to tuck myself into bed. When I finally did, the phone rang.

"I wanted to say good-night and wish you pleasant dreams. I'll call you in the morning."

Stephen was still full of surprises. And in the morning, he called again just like he said he would. He was romantic, sweet, and reliable, too. And that kiss . . . I smiled at the thought.

It was Sunday, a chance to linger over coffee and read the paper before taking a shower. Some friends were having a barbeque across the street, but it had already been a long weekend and what I really wanted was to stay in and get some rest. They'd been so kind and welcoming ever since I'd moved to the neighborhood, so I popped over for a brief hello and a quick bite before making my excuses and heading home.

The answering machine was flickering away as I walked back in. "Call you later," Stephen had said.

It had to be a dream, a man so attentive and kind? I wondered how long he could keep it up, or how long before we tired of each other. I wasn't any good at relationships and I'd gained almost a hundred pounds after the last break-up. Losing it was like climbing a mountain in sandals; long, slow, and just about impossible. I thought of telling Stephen that I didn't want to see him again, but that was just as scary. It seemed I was stuck.

Stephen called again later that day. "Just checking in," he said. "I'm still at my sister's house." He'd already told his family all about me. "They can't wait to meet you, honey. And I can't wait to introduce you."

"It's a little too soon, Stephen. I hope you understand. I'm not ready for that."

NEVER SAY NEVER

"That's okay for now, but before long you'll be sitting around the table with us. Mark my words."

The next evening, Stephen and I were toasting over chicken parmesan, clicking wine glass against soda. I chuckled under my breath at the assurance I had that he'd never become a nasty drunk. He didn't drink.

We'd been laughing and talking throughout the dinner, but behind the banter was a layer of sadness. Stephen had noticed and asked what was wrong. I explained about my little feline friend, Woofer. He hadn't been acting right and I was concerned about him. The vet had taken tests earlier that day, but results weren't due back until tomorrow. When I explained my concern for Woofer's health, Stephen kindly offered to finish the evening in my living room, so I could keep an eye on Woofer.

He was compassionate in addition to all his other fine traits, and he had a heart for animals, too. "We'll take care of this together," he said. "Everything will be all right."

He showered my little Woofer with attention, caring for him as though he were a sick child. The next day when I called to check on the test results, the vet asked me to come in. This couldn't be good, I thought.

"Woofer has leukemia," the veterinarian announced, startling me with the diagnosis.

"What?" I asked.

"It's leukemia," he repeated.

He prescribed medication and told me to bring Woofer back in a few days for more testing. Stephen was ready to come over the minute I called him with the news.

"No, thank you. I really appreciate it, but it's late and I need to get some sleep."

I tossed and turned throughout the night, trying not to think about the diagnosis. "C'mon, God," I called out. "Haven't I been through enough?"

I decided the diagnosis couldn't have been right. I'd find another vet. Three thousand dollars later, Woofer's diagnosis was the same and the prognosis dismal. In the end, I was faced with a decision no one wants to make.

"Stephen, I need help," I told him over the phone.

Stephen accompanied me to the vet who explained how he'd done everything possible and it was now at a point where he was concerned about the pain Woofer was experiencing. "It's only going to get worse," he said.

I ran from the room crying. Stephen came after me and turned my face to his. "We'll get through this together," he promised.

No, I couldn't get through this. Not after everything I'd already been through. I just wanted to curl up and die. I tried to speak in between sobs. "I don't want him to suffer. I love him too much for that. But I just can't lose him. I can't."

"Celeste, I know you love him and you've done everything you possibly could, but he's suffering now and there's only one thing you can do to help him. Honey, it's going to take courage and a whole lot of love, but you have to let him go."

Stephen held me while I cried. When I brought my head up, I wiped my eyes and nodded in consent. Together, we walked back into the office and I signed the papers.

After that, Stephen took me home to clean up Woofer's things, but I just couldn't face it and broke down again.

"Let's go shopping," he suggested. "A little distraction never hurt anyone." We walked arm-in-arm around the mall, stopping at a kiosk where Stephen bought me a little stuffed animal couple, hugging. It was very sweet the way he had our names engraved onto a little bar that they were holding. Then, once we were home, he helped me to gather Woofer's toys and food bowl, taking them out to the trash for me. It was one of my roughest days, and the weeks that followed were long and hollow. My little companion, Woofer, was gone and I was alone again.

Stephen and I continued seeing each other, taking things slowly, as we each dealt with what we had to. After visiting Stephen at his

NEVER SAY NEVER

apartment in Bayside, one day, I returned home to a message from the vet. It had been weeks since Woofer had passed and I couldn't imagine why he was calling. When I called back, he asked if I'd come by to meet a friend of his. Out of curiosity, I agreed. When I arrived at his office, later that day, his friend was sitting on the desk meowing.

"Isn't he cute? I checked him from top to bottom and he's in perfect health, but he's a little sad because he needs a loving home. I was wondering if you knew anyone who might be able to provide one." His eyebrows rose, as he waited for me to answer.

"Well, I must admit, I had thought of getting a kitten, but I wasn't sure if I was ready." I took the little Calico into my arms and fell in love. Still, I wasn't sure if I could make the necessary commitment. "Can I have a day to think it over?"

"Of course," he said. "We'll talk tomorrow."

I was sad for the little guy, but things were busy at work and with my personal life, so I wasn't sure if I had the time to take care of a kitten. I was doing a lot of traveling for business and spending a lot of time with Stephen. There was way too much going on to take on additional responsibility, so I called the vet to thank him, but declined.

Later on that week my sister's dog had passed away. The vet had called her and left a message that he had the dog's collar and Theresa could come by and get it any time. I knew how hard it would be for her to go in and get it. It was the same vet I'd used and they knew me, so I volunteered to go for her.

The moment I walked through the door I saw the little Calico. His crate was smack in the middle of the waiting room and he was meowing so sweetly. Talk about impulse shopping! I grabbed both Calico and the collar and went home.

He was adorable, running all over the place, acclimating himself to his new environment. Stephen came over to see him and before the night was through they were inseparable. There was no doubt that bringing the kitten home had been the right decision.

And so was accepting Stephen's proposal. He had said from the beginning he was going to marry me, and he was right. As the months passed, Stephen and I tried to make plans for our wedding, but we were just getting back on our feet after some financial setbacks. Both our bank accounts were seriously depleted and we really couldn't see any way to afford a wedding unless we hit the lottery. Theresa offered to help us. She said we could live in her downstairs apartment, for a modest rent, and save for the wedding. We jumped at the opportunity and managed to save enough money for a beautiful, black tie wedding in a very short time.

Finally, fate had rewarded me with something greater than money could buy. I walked down the aisle in a white satin gown. Stephen was dressed in tails, waiting by the altar. He never looked more handsome.

"With this ring, I thee wed." The words were as sweet as any nectar and my heart swelled with joy as we promised to love one another . . . 'til death do us part.

CHAPTER THIRTY-ONE

We had a house built in Medford, Long Island and began the life I'd always dreamed of having. My marriage to Stephen had added stability to my world. Stephen was my anchor. He was the voice of reason with the ability to keep me calm through any situation. I'd hoped he could also do the same for Keith, helping him to feel safe enough to open his heart. But I was disappointed when Keith's feelings remained as reserved as they'd always been. Still, I was certain that one day he'd find his own special someone who would be able to unlock his heart. I looked forward to that day and hoped the warmth generated by those new feelings would spill over onto me as well.

Keith was eighteen when the call came, his voice bubbling over with exuberance. "Mom, there's someone I want you to meet."

Mary was from Long Island, but she attended college upstate at Binghamton University. They'd met during the summer while working at the park. When he brought her to meet us, Stephen and I fought back smiles as Mary nervously clung to Keith's side. The two were clearly taken with each other, enough to undertake the formalities of parental introductions.

When the summer was over, Keith followed her upstate. We weren't thrilled with his choice and suggested Mary would do better in school if he stayed here and visited her on weekends and holidays. After all, she was in her senior year and needed to concentrate on her studies.

Surprisingly enough, Keith agreed to do as we suggested, continuing to work for the parks department until Mary had finished school. At least that's what Keith led us to believe. When I went to visit him at work as I sometimes did, I found out he didn't work there anymore. I tracked him down on his cell and he explained that he'd been one of the first to get cut after the summer.

"Let me see if I can find you another job," I told him. "Why don't we meet for dinner tonight?" Keith was evasive and non-committal, which just added to my suspicion. There were too many things that just didn't line up. It was only a few weeks ago when he'd said the parks department wanted him to stay on after the summer. He'd said most of their staff had gone back to school. No, this just didn't make any sense.

I met with one of the supervisors who knew me from the many times I had stopped by to see Keith. "What happened," I asked.

"Celeste," she looked me squarely in the eye, "Keith resigned. We asked him to stay on, but he said he couldn't."

"Thank you; I appreciate your time and candor." As I was leaving I ran into a co-worker of Keith's. We chatted briefly and he asked me how Keith was doing.

"Actually, I thought he was still working here."

"Keith left weeks ago," he said. "I thought he went upstate with his girlfriend."

"Excuse me? He went where?" My mouth opened in shock and I was stunned. One look at me and he realized I had no idea. He told me that Keith and Mary were going to stay near her school until she graduated, and then they planned to look for a house around the area.

"It didn't sound like a secret," he said. "I figured you knew."

The pieces were starting to fit together and what a picture it was. Keith had lied because we didn't agree with his choice. I called Stephen immediately and he didn't seem that shocked.

"You probably would have done the same thing if you were in his shoes. Don't you think?"

Stephen was always the voice of reason.

"Celeste, you need to think this through before you call him. Give it a day or two. We'll talk more about it later. Okay?"

"That's why I love you, Stephen."

"Why?"

"Because you're so smart. See you soon."

Unfortunately, Keith was not privy to our conversation and called just as I was walking into the house. It took great restraint, but I took Stephen's advice and didn't say a word. We limited our conversation to small talk, and then I told him I'd call him the next day.

The following day, after further discussion with Stephen and a good night's sleep, I decided further investigation was warranted. I called Keith's father to find out what he knew.

"Keith went upstate to be with Mary," he said, surprised that I was asking.

"Why didn't you tell me?"

"I assumed you knew."

"No, I didn't. I found out the hard way, purely by accident."

After talking to Rob, I telephoned Keith and confronted him with the situation.

"I'm more than a little disappointed that you lied to me. I didn't appreciate finding out the way I did."

"Mom, you would never have agreed. I was going to tell you, but I was waiting for the right time."

"What about Mary's parents? Do they know?"

"They also just found out."

"And?"

"And they're not happy, but they know they can't do anything about it."

"Do you think they'll approve of your relationship when you're disrespecting their wishes by living together?"

"Mom, we don't care who approves. Mary and I love each other and we want to be together. No one's going to stop us."

"Well, Keith, I hope you know what you're doing."

Keith and I spoke on a fairly regular basis after that, but he knew I was less than pleased with his decision and it did put a strain on our relationship. Still, from time to time he'd call for a word of advice, but it never seemed to be what he wanted to hear and eventually he stopped calling altogether. Despite my attempts to contact him it was several months before he called again.

"Mom, we're coming down for Thanksgiving."

"Will you be joining us for dinner then," I asked.

"No, we already have plans with Mary's family, but I'll call when I'm in."

Keith phoned on Thanksgiving and I invited him over for drinks and hors d'oeuvres before dinner. When he declined I suggested dessert. He accepted the invitation for dessert, but he never showed up. Every time I tried his cell, it went immediately to voicemail.

He finally called just as we were getting ready for bed.

"Keith, where you are? What happened? Are you okay? And why didn't you come over?"

"I'm sorry, Mom. We got caught up with something and the time just flew by."

"You could've called," I said. "We were worried. And very disappointed."

He apologized and offered to come for a visit the next day.

"Of course, we'll have lunch, or dinner; whichever you like."

"Great! I'll call you in the morning." I went to sleep with a smile that night, excited that I was going to see Keith the next day."

In the morning, I went shopping for every one of Keith's favorites. No matter which meal he chose, I was going to be prepared. But while I was out, Keith had left a message they were taking Mary's nephew somewhere and he'd call me later. Immediately, I phoned him. He said he wasn't sure anymore if they'd even be able to make it.

"It was unexpected. I'm sorry," he said.

The next day Keith was on our doorstep. It was an unplanned visit and he was alone. I fixed a snack for him and we talked a while, but he didn't stay long because he was expected back at Mary's parent's house. The following day they were on their way back upstate.

We hardly heard a word from Keith until after Mary graduated. Mary's parents had withdrawn their financial support after

NEVER SAY NEVER

she graduated and both Mary and Keith were forced to return to Long Island.

The two were miserable apart. Keith was living with Rob again and Mary went back home to her parents. But before long Rob's delinquent finances had caught up with him and he lost the house. Keith was thrilled when Rob decided to move out of state because it gave him a legitimate reason to be with Mary again. I had hoped he would come and live with us, but he moved in with Mary's family the minute they extended an invitation.

I desperately looked for opportunities to help Keith shape his life into something with a promising future, but he never gave me the chance. Though disappointed, I assured him that I would always be there for him whether I agreed with his choices or not.

The following week, Keith called to share his good news. He had found an apartment. It was a step toward independence and I was pleased. Mary, he quickly added, would be staying over on weekends.

I continued to invite Keith and Mary to go out with us or to come over, anything that meant spending time together, but with or without Mary it was close to impossible. In the meantime, I resigned myself to phone conversations whenever he was willing, while holding out hope for more.

A year later, when his lease expired, Keith and Mary moved back upstate. They found jobs and an apartment in Ballston Spa; a charming town, rich in history, and minutes from downtown Saratoga Springs. It was a four hour drive from Long Island, but distance was irrelevant since Stephen and I hardly saw them anyway. A phone call was a phone call. It didn't make much difference where it originated.

Keith and Mary were very happy. They managed to make it down for the holidays, but never seemed to find time to come over to our house and visit. There was always an excuse. I was just explaining my feelings to Keith when Mary grabbed the phone from him. She was certainly in for a rude awakening. I let her know exactly what I thought about her little manipulations.

"Keith never gets an opportunity to see his family because you make it impossible. You're always asking him to make plans with your family and you give us excuses. Are you that needy, or so insecure that you can't let him spend any time with us?" When I was through, I told her she'd better put my son back on the phone or I would go over there and rip her hair right from her head. I think I added a few words about burying her in the dirt where even dogs wouldn't find her. It was something like that. When Keith came on the line I continued my tirade, telling him he had better inform the little witch that our conversations did not include an open invitation for her to join in. "She'd better know her place and stay there before I put her in it."

Keith was not too happy about what I'd said. He threatened to never speak to me again unless I apologized to her. Well, I was so enraged by her audacity to say that we were not available for them that I flat out refused. Then, I laced into him about Mary's interference in our relationship.

I was through accommodating their lack of respect or consideration. When Keith was ready to stand up to Mary and spend some time with his family, he could let me know. Until then, I had no interest in talking to either one of them.

It was a little over a year when Keith finally called. We played catch-up, dishing up all the news from the time we had missed. He sounded excited as he told me all about how Mary's parents had helped them with a down payment on a small house. A new beginning had emerged for us that day and I was grateful to have my son back in my life.

We spoke regularly for a while, but we were both so busy the calls dwindled down and we eventually lost contact again. When I realized how long it had been since I'd heard from him I made the call. That's when I discovered his phone had been disconnected.

Keith and I had formed our patterns long ago. It may not have been an active choice, but it certainly was a consequence of our actions.

When he called the next time, I hardly recognized his voice.

"Keith? Is that you?"

NEVER SAY NEVER

"Yeah, Mom, it's me."

"Keith, what's wrong? Where are you? Are you okay?" The questions came one after the other.

"I have some news, Mom."

"Good news, I hope."

"Well, some good and some bad. Which do you want first?"

"Whichever you want to give me."

"Where's Stephen?"

"He's right here."

"Okay, I'll tell you what's going on."

"Keith, what's wrong? I'm getting worried."

"I have cancer."

"What?"

"They think it's treatable."

"Thank, God!"

"Mom, it's stage four melanoma."

"Keith, start at the beginning and tell me the whole story. And please don't leave anything out."

"It started three months ago as a mole on my back, but it was kind of raw and started to bleed, so I went to the doctor. He gave me some ointment and said it wasn't a big deal, nothing I needed to worry about. He mentioned that I could get a second opinion, but since he didn't think it was anything I didn't see why I needed one. After a while, I decided to go for that second opinion because I wasn't sure it was healing right, even with the ointment. That dermatologist took a biopsy, just to be safe. Anyway, it came back positive. They took more and sent it out again. Based on the results, he recommended a surgeon who explained the situation. Mom, he said it was cancer, stage four."

"Keith, listen. This is serious. I want some phone numbers. I need to get to the bottom of this. I'm not comfortable that all the information is clear and accurate. I would like to talk to these doctors myself."

"No, Mom, please. I want to take care of this on my own. There's no mistake. This is what's happening. Mary and I just got the news ourselves and I haven't had much time to digest it yet. Please, just give me some time to think."

My voice started to crack at the sound of his plea. At least he couldn't see the tears.

"Mom, I need you to be strong for me. Okay? I don't want you to worry. I'll be fine."

"Of course, you will. You're my son. You'll get through this with flying colors."

"Mary and I are going away for a few days. I'll call you when we get back."

"Where are you going?"

"Mom, I'll call you when we get back."

"Keith, you can't just leave. We need to deal with this."

"You can call the doctors and I'll speak to you soon. I'll leave authorization for you to talk to them." Keith had relented and given me the numbers. It was a small consolation, but it was something.

"I love you, Keith."

"I love you too, Mom."

Stephen could tell something was seriously wrong. "Do you want to fill me in?" he asked the minute I hung up the phone. I repeated the entire story for him, every single word.

Giving Keith a chance to set up the authorizations, I waited until morning to make the calls. To my surprise, Keith's internist wasn't even aware of the situation, other than the fact Keith had gone to a dermatologist for a second opinion.

"You failed at your job and now my son is fighting for his life."

"I'm very sorry Mrs. Roth, but I assure you I took appropriate steps based on the information before me. And I did tell Keith that he was welcome to get another opinion."

The next call was to the dermatologist. She explained Keith's condition and spent a great deal of time on the phone with me.

"Moles are not always so easy to diagnose. They can be deceiving. I've learned it's better to be safe and have a biopsy, unless I'm one-hundred-percent sure it's nothing. In Keith's case, it looked suspicious. That's why I sent it out for pathology. Keith's already been to the surgeon I recommended, but I'm not passing him off; I'm staying close to this case. Your son is a wonderful young man and we're going to do everything we can to help him."

The next call was to the surgeon.

"We're going to do everything we can, Mrs. Roth." He explained about the procedure he had discussed with Keith. "Until we see exactly which areas are affected I can't tell you very much. The only thing I can say with certainty is that we need to move on this right away."

Stephen and I spent hours talking it through, trying to get an emotional grip on the situation. As usual, Stephen was the voice of reason. What he said was very similar to what the surgeon had said, but coming from Stephen it sounded less ominous. "We'll just have to be patient until the surgeon sees how extensively the cancer has spread before we can formulate a plan of attack." He was right, of course, but all I knew was that I was not going to let Keith die.

After a few days without hearing from Keith I started to get worried. Mary's mother, also alarmed, had called to ask if I'd heard from them.

"Mary usually checks in and least once a day, even if it's just for a quick hello. This is so unlike her," she said.

I tried the number Keith had called from the last time, but there was no answer. Mary's mother tried a few numbers, also without much success. Frantic the news had been more than they could bear; I called the local police and explained the situation, asking if they could send someone to check on them.

Keith's call came an hour later. "Hi, Mom."

"Keith? Where have you been? It's been three days. I was worried sick."

"Yeah, I figured you were worried when the police showed up." He laughed. "Only you could get the police to check on your son."

"A worried mother has great power. Don't ever forget that."

Two weeks later, I paced the lobby of St. Peter's Hospital in Albany where Keith was scheduled to undergo a four hour procedure.

"Take it easy, Mom. You're wearing the shine off the floor." he said. "It'll be fine, you'll see."

I gave him the biggest hug I could muster. "Of course it will. These people have heard of my reputation and they don't want to have to deal with me." I grinned and planted a big kiss on his cheek. "Now let's get this behind us. Go!" I commanded.

Like defendants on trial, Mary and I sat waiting for the verdict. We tried small talk, encouragement, and finally silence. Six hours passed with no news, not a word. Tears trickled. I blotted them with a tissue. By the end of the eighth hour, I was inconsolable.

The nurse came out and tried to calm me. "They're finished," she said. "Everything's fine. You can see Keith in about an hour."

"Thank you," I sniffled. She directed us to the third floor and showed us a waiting room where the surgeon would come and talk to us. Just as we walked in, he came through the door.

"Everything went well," he said. "It looks like we got it all."

"Thank you, doctor." Tears of relief rolled down my cheeks.

"Keith's in recovery. He'll be able to go home in a few hours. He'll have to check in with the oncologist in a few days. Other than that, it looks good."

I followed him down the hall. "Doctor, I need to know the truth. What are his chances?"

"I'd say they were about sixty/forty. Keith is young and strong. That's important. Be positive and give him all the support he needs. You can speak with his oncologist in a few days and she'll have more information for you then."

If anyone could beat this it was Keith. The odds weren't great, but they were in his favor.

A couple of hours later Keith had eaten Jello, soup, and managed to polish off a meatball hero. I wasn't sure he should be stuffing himself like that so soon after the procedure, but the nurse had said, "If he wants it, give it to him."

NEVER SAY NEVER

Keith was discharged within a few hours and Mary drove the three of us back to their house. We did make one stop on the way. Keith was still hungry, so we got him something at McDonalds. I'd never seen anything like it. I took it as a good sign and didn't say anything else. Keith had gone to lie down for a while, but he was up before long and eating a bowl of cereal. Seeing him eat like that reassured me more than any words.

"Is the couch okay, Mom, or would you rather have my bed?" Keith asked.

"Listen, you get some sleep. I'll be just fine," I assured him. Where I slept was the least of my concerns.

Sunshine was soon filtering through the blinds and Keith was already up fixing breakfast for all of us.

"I should be making breakfast for you," I said.

"Don't be silly, Mom, you're a guest."

"Mother's are never guests. They do for their children, anywhere, anytime." I put my slippers on. "Keith, you just had surgery. Let me do that."

"Mom, please. I want to make breakfast."

"Fine, go ahead, make breakfast."

Keith fixed everything from bacon and eggs to muffins with jam. He even cut up fresh fruit. After breakfast, we all got ready and Keith took us around town to see some of the sights.

I treated the kids to dinner out that evening, and then the next morning I slipped out extra early to buy fresh bagels and muffins before anyone was awake. We did a little shopping together, and then Keith took me to the train. With my eyes safely hidden behind sunglasses, I said good-bye and gave him a big hug. Then, I hurried onto the train before the tears had a chance to slip below the frames.

"Call me when you get home," he shouted after me.

"Who's the mother now?" I smiled.

137

CHAPTER THIRTY-TWO

My dislike for Mary had turned to gratitude. Her love for my son was evident. I had no doubt that she would see him through this horrendous ordeal. Even so, periodically, I took the long ride upstate to check on them.

Keith's latest screens indicated he was cancer free. Other than the daily injections of interferon there was no evidence of illness at all. Still, his oncologist remained guarded about long term recovery. She suggested I read up on melanoma.

"You need to understand what we're dealing with," she'd said.

Mary and Keith continued working, moving their lives forward. Mary managed a group home for young adults with challenges. Keith worked with a similar population at another location, happily giving of himself.

It took much longer than I would have liked, but Keith and I had a good relationship now. He called every week to tell me about work and the different things he was doing. I was absolutely thrilled when he told me he'd realized that his earning capacity wasn't enough to provide for a family, especially if Mary wanted to stay home and raise children. He was thinking about his future and considering school as a possibility, or even an apprenticeship program. My son was growing up.

Keith had undergone some routine blood work and a PET scan to confirm that he was still in remission, but waiting for the results was driving them crazy. They decided the best thing to do would be to drive down to Florida and visit Mary's parents who had been spending the winter months in the warm weather. The distraction would be just what they needed, helping to pass the time as they waited for news.

Keith's cell phone rang shortly after they arrived. From the sound of the doctor's voice he knew it wasn't good. The cancer had spread to his liver. She'd assured him there were still some treatment options they could try when he returned.

I was the first call Keith made after he hung up with the doctor. "Mom, the cancer's spread." I was devastated, but tried my best to remain positive.

"Everything is going to work out. I promise. Do you hear me? You just relax and know in your heart that things will be okay. We beat this before; we can do it again." I put Stephen on the phone with Keith and he also gave him all the reasons to keep on believing.

Keith called again the next day. He and Mary were married. "Please don't be upset. We wanted to do this by ourselves. I hope you and Stephen understand."

"Of course, I would have loved to see my son get married, but I understand and I'm happy for both of you."

CHAPTER THIRTY-THREE

When Keith and Mary returned from Florida, he was admitted to Albany University Hospital for a clinical trial. I'd done extensive research on the subject, as the oncologist had suggested, and I knew about the statistics. Fewer than three percent of melanoma patients survived and the treatments themselves had many side effects. It wasn't promising, but my resolve was set. Keith would be one of the miracles. I went to the hospital prepared to be a tower of strength for my son.

I stayed for the first few days, but when the treatment actually began Keith and Mary said they wanted to handle it by themselves. How could I argue? Keith had already found what had taken me an eternity to find, someone to love, someone who would stand by him no matter what. It seemed ironic that in order to give my son what he needed most, I had to leave again.

My resolve cracked the moment the train pulled out of the station. I cried the whole way home.

"Celeste, we'll get him through this together," Stephen said when we talked later that day. It was hard for him, too, but as always he was my anchor and dutifully fulfilled his role offering words of hope and love."

Keith called a few days later.

"Are you still at work?" he asked.

"Where else would I be?"

He laughed and said, "Go home already. You need to get some rest."

"It's not that late. Don't worry about me. I live for this!" I asked him about his day and told him I spoke to the doctor and that everything was going according to plan. He was glad I was on top of things. He knew I had his best interest at heart and was relentless in making sure he had excellent care. In a way, it was through this tragedy that Keith discovered the best parts of me. He appreciated the way I fought for him, running over anyone I had to in the process. If only we could've gotten to this place some other way . . . But I'd learned a long time ago that life just wasn't fair.

Keith wanted to know when I planned on coming up next.

"In a couple of weeks," I said, "unless you'd like me to come sooner."

"No, we may have to push it off. I have to go to New Hampshire for the next round of treatment. It's very intense and only available at certain hospitals. It'll take a full week and they'll be monitoring me the whole time."

Of course I volunteered to go along, but Keith and Mary wanted to do it alone. I was content that Keith knew I was there for him. Still, I couldn't just sit around and do nothing, so I set out on a mission to purchase some essentials for him. I combed the stores for comfortable sweats, pajamas, and even some new underwear. I needed to be able to care for him somehow, even if only in this small way.

I took everything I'd gotten and packed it all in a box. Then, I took the box to the post office and sent it off to Keith. I called every single day to see if the package had arrived, but it still hadn't shown up. This was ridiculous! It was already the day before he was scheduled to leave. I'd mailed it in plenty of time. Someone was not doing their job. I called the post office near Keith's house and frantically explained the situation.

"You have to find the package," I demanded. "My son needs these things." My tone grew desperate, bordering hysterical. "He's going into the hospital. Please, he's very ill. It's imperative that you find it."

They found the package the morning Keith was scheduled to leave, but explained that it couldn't be delivered until the next day.

NEVER SAY NEVER

"No. That can't be. My son has cancer. He's leaving for the hospital. Please, he needs these things... The treatment..." And I continued to explain all of the reasons why the package had to be delivered immediately.

"Let me see what I can do. I'll call you back in a few minutes."

Twenty minutes later, Keith called. "Mom, you're relentless!" he said in a voice tinged with laughter.

"Why?" I asked.

"Because you are the only person that could get the Post Master General to deliver a package at eight o'clock in the morning."

"Hallelujah! I was so worried it wouldn't get there in time."

"The guy wanted to know if you were really my mother. I was almost too embarrassed to admit it, but I said, that's my mother all right."

He said, "It's lucky for you, young man, she's on your side."

"So now the police and the postal service know my mother and do her bidding."

We laughed for a good ten minutes over that.

"Mom, I know we've had our differences in the past, but I'm really glad to have you on my side. I know you'll fight for me with everything you have. I love you for that."

Those were the sweetest words I'd ever heard. Tears of joy trickled down my cheeks. "I love you, too, Keith, for ever and ever."

When I told him the post office story, Stephen laughed so hard his sides cramped. He looked at me with a mixture of love and admiration, which was exactly how I viewed him.

My husband was very aware that nothing would stand in my way when I had a goal to accomplish. On some occasions he'd even help.

Keith called later that evening when he was settled into his room, awaiting his first treatment. He said everyone was just wonderful and they even brought in a bed in for Mary, so she could stay with him.

"Don't worry, Mom."

"Me worry? Don't be silly. I love you, Keith."

"Love you, too, Mom."

Keith called again the next day. He'd had his second treatment and was tired. He wanted to sleep, so we didn't stay on long, but I felt better after hearing his voice. By the third day, he was so exhausted I could barely hear him. Mary explained how the treatment was taking a toll on his body. He'd started convulsing during his last treatment, but the staff was monitoring him every step of the way. They said it was nothing to worry about, but they'd see how he handled the next treatment.

"If you need me, I can come," I told Mary.

"No thank you; we're okay. We'll keep you posted."

Keith needed a few more treatments before being released, but I wasn't sure if I was getting the whole story accurately. When Keith called he was still weak. He said the treatments were getting tougher but he would be okay. I was never so proud of my boy. What fortitude! There was no denying he was his mother's son.

Keith continued the treatments and either he or Mary called every day. As the days progressed, Mary sounded worried. I pressed for answers but there were none. Keith took the phone and tried to talk, but I couldn't understand much of what he was saying, except for two words, "I'm okay."

Finally, out of my mind with worry, I called the nurses station to find out what was going on.

"Everything's fine Mrs. Roth. What Keith is experiencing is all normal and his strength will return soon enough," his nurse assured me.

Mary called later and said he was okay, but wouldn't eat. She said they weren't going to do the final treatment because Keith wasn't strong enough. They didn't think his body could take another round. When Keith called later we were able to talk for a little while, but he was still very weak. He said they'd be discharging him at the end of the week.

Keith went home to rest and Mary's mother came to help out. Rob was on his way in from Minnesota and arrived just after Mary's mother left. He stayed for a month. By the time he left, Keith and

NEVER SAY NEVER

Mary were ready for some time alone, so Stephen and I waited a while before visiting.

In the interim, Keith had met with the oncologist. His spirits tanked when the news wasn't good. Stephen and I rushed right up there to find out what was going on. Over lunch, Keith told us the details of the report.

"Mom, it was weird the way he wanted to know if I had made any plans. Like for my death or something. It really shook me up. How can they talk like that?"

"Some people are just stupid, Keith. They can be very insensitive. Obviously, that oncologist is in the wrong profession. We can't take to heart what stupid people say. The world's full of them."

We spent the rest of the afternoon shopping, and then went out for a nice dinner. The day turned around and ended on a hopeful note, but first thing the next morning I called the oncologist we had been dealing with from the beginning.

"I'd like to know who would talk to my son like that. How can someone just rip the hope right out of my son's heart? Why would someone do that?"

"I was afraid that would happen at some point. That particular oncologist is in charge of the treatment center. He's one of the best in the country, but not well versed in bedside manner. Unfortunately, insensitive people sometimes become insensitive doctors. I'll talk to Keith. Have him call me."

As we pulled out of the driveway and headed home, I told Stephen I was worried I might not see Keith again. He pulled the car over to the side and took my hands in his. "Keith is going to make it. Understand?"

I just nodded.

CHAPTER THIRTY-FOUR

Thanksgiving was approaching and I thought about Keith coming down to spend some time with his in-laws, and then with us, too. After that, there'd be Christmas and we'd go back up to visit with them. It took a few days, but I convinced myself there'd be plenty of time to spend together. Keith was not done yet. Not by a long shot.

Keith called every day looking for some way to put things into perspective. Although I was happy for the frequent calls, it broke my heart that he was so anxious. I wanted him to feel secure, to believe without a doubt that he was going to get well. He looked wonderful when I saw him for Thanksgiving. You'd never know he was sick. When they went back home, he called again, fearful, losing all the ground we'd made during our visit.

"C'mon, Keith, listen to me. You are going to be fine," I insisted.

"But the odds, Mom, they're not good."

"Statistics mean nothing. They're just a bunch of numbers. You look great and you feel great. So believe that you are great! Okay?"

"Thanks, Mom. It always helps when I talk to you."

I hated that he was so scared and I did my best to build him up and leave him with a sense of hope. Still, I couldn't shake the sense that time was running out. I wouldn't voice it, but inside the dread was there, the days ticking away, never knowing which was going to be the last.

Christmas came and went and Keith looked fabulous. He ate with vigor. Maybe the doctors were wrong. Maybe he would be one of the lucky ones, the less than three percent.

Mary's sister took the train up and stayed with them for New

Year's. Mary's parent's spent time with them after that, and then it was my turn again.

When all the holiday visiting was done, we gave them a break. They needed some time to recover from the whirlwind of houseguests. By Easter, Mary was ready to entertain again. She made a lovely dinner and afterward Keith and I drove to the bakery for some sweets. I'd hoped he would eat some sticky, sweet baked goods because he'd hardly eaten a thing at dinner. Without saying a word, I watched as he moved the food around on his plate, never actually putting anything in his mouth. His once ravenous appetite had waned considerably and he began to lose some weight. Still, he looked pretty good considering the treatments and everything he was going through. Maybe he'd eat a donut, an éclair, something, anything . . . I'd hoped.

We stayed overnight and left the following morning after a huge breakfast. Keith was starting another round of treatment, but we promised to come back when he was finished.

As the aggressive treatment took its toll, I scolded Keith over the phone. "You have to eat! You have to keep your strength up."

"Okay, Mom, just for you."

Keith's independence was very important to him and he continued to drive himself to and from appointments. It was a trait I understood all too well, probably one that led straight back to me.

"Mom, the tumor went away. The treatment's working."

I screamed, smiled, and cried. Could this be the miracle we'd been waiting for? I called Stephen the minute we hung up.

Next, I dialed the oncologist. I needed to hear it from her. She was very happy for Keith, but cautiously optimistic. "It's important that we continue his treatments and monitor his condition. We should all continue to be hopeful, but understand we haven't beaten this yet."

Keith's treatments continued for a while, but then stopped again. His body could only tolerate so much. They took blood the following week and unfortunately didn't see any improvement. The disease was spreading.

NEVER SAY NEVER

Keith needed to get away from the hospitals, the sickness, everything, so we invited him and Mary down to spend some time with us. It was all set for the first week of June. Stephen and I were so excited. It had been almost two months since we'd seen him and we could hardly wait. "Be prepared to eat," I told Keith. "I'm going to plump you up."

A couple of nights later, Keith's oncologist called me. "We just got Keith's blood work back and it's not good."

"What do you mean?"

"You need to prepare yourself, Celeste. Keith is at the end. He doesn't have much time." My knees buckled and I fell to the floor.

Stephen rushed to my side, lifting me onto a chair. "What's wrong? Who is that?"

I couldn't speak. I just handed him the phone.

"Hello?"

Stephen's face turned ashen as the doctor repeated the heartbreaking news.

"What can we do for him?" He asked if Keith knew.

"I understand. Thank you, doctor." He hung up the phone and looked at me, his eyes mirroring the pain in my own. He leaned against the counter, his chin dropping to his chest.

I took a long, deep breath and let it out slowly. Stephen opened his arms to me and I walked into them, laying my head against his chest. Together we cried.

Sadness gave way to madness as I tried desperately to reach, first, Keith, and then Mary. There was no answer on either of their phones.

How could this happen? It just wasn't fair. I couldn't deal with this. It was too much. I was already on medication to get through the illness; it wasn't strong enough to get through loss. But I couldn't think about that now. Keith needed me and I had to stay strong for him.

When Keith finally called back he could hear the alarm in my voice. "Honey, where are you? Are you okay? I've been trying to get a hold of you." I didn't want to add to what he was already carrying, so I didn't say anything about the call from his oncologist, but he suddenly blurted it out.

"Mom, I was at the doctor's office today. She asked if I'd made any arrangements. I asked her why she was saying that. She said she was just wondering."

"Keith, doctors have said that before. You know it doesn't mean anything."

"Mom, I'm not sure what she was talking about, but I left and I really don't want to think about it anymore right now."

"Okay, honey. But try to remember that sometimes things come out wrong. It was probably just one of those times." I couldn't let him give up. Not when we still had plenty of fight left in us.

Keith called again a few days later. He and Mary were on their way down to see us. "Stephen, they'll be here soon," I yelled with excitement.

When they pulled into the driveway Stephen and I ran out to greet them. Keith was in the passenger seat. Mary walked around to help him out. I almost collapsed when I saw him. He'd lost so much weight. He was so frail that he could hardly walk. I wanted to cry, but I forced myself to go over and give him a big kiss.

"Come, c'mon in. I'll get some blankets to make the couch a little more comfortable for you."

"Thanks, Mom."

Stephen and I gathered up all the blankets we could find and brought them out to the sofa, hoping to cushion him enough to lessen the pain, even just a little. We did our best to help him get comfortable, and then I excused myself and went to the kitchen.

I leaned over the counter, holding on for dear life. We had no idea. They'd never said a word. We never imagined… I swallowed hard, then poured a glass of juice and took it in to Keith. He gave me a little smile, as best as he could. He was weak and his speech was labored, but he seemed genuinely happy to be with us.

I thought about the fact that Keith had traveled all that way, in pain. My son, I'd realized, had come home to die.

NEVER SAY NEVER

It was obvious the last few months had taken a huge toll on Mary as well. She looked tired and worn. She mentioned that she'd like to visit with a girlfriend, so Keith asked if we'd mind if she went.

"Of course not," I said to Mary. "Take some time for yourself. We'll stay with Keith." Mary said she would check in later and told us to call if we needed her for anything.

Keith wanted to see the photos that were all around the room, on walls and in bookcases, so he slowly lifted himself to a standing position and inched his way around looking at photos, smiling at the memories.

I excused myself again and went into the kitchen to phone Rob.

"You have to get out here right away," I told him. "Keith's here. He's in really bad shape. You need to come right now. There isn't much time."

"I know. Mary called us. We've rented a car. We'll be there in three days."

"Rob, I'm not sure he has three days." I hung up the phone and ran outside. Reality had hit me like a hot iron. I fell to my knees, buried my face in my hands, and sobbed so hard I was afraid I wouldn't be able to breathe.

Keith was waiting, so I somehow managed to pull myself together. I quickly fixed my face before going back in to see him. The last thing he needed was for me to fall apart.

He turned to me as I walked into the living room. "It's not fair, Mom. Why me? Why is this happening?"

"You listen to me, Keith." I took his face gently between my hands. "This is not about fair. It's not about how good or bad you are. This is an illness and you have to believe that you'll beat it. This is just the aftermath of the chemo. Do you understand? Give yourself some time to get your strength back." I couldn't tell him he was going to die. How could I say that when I didn't want to accept it myself?

I cradled him in my arms as he cried on my shoulder.

Keith probably needed to be in the hospital, but we decided he was better off at home with us. Mary had called to see if we'd mind if she spent the night at her friend's house.

"You've been there for Keith every step of the way. You deserve a night off. Relax and have a good time. We'll call you if anything comes up."

Stephen and I offered Keith our bed, but he wouldn't hear of it.

"The couch is just fine, Mom. I like the den, especially the big TV." I turned the television on for him and made sure he had a channel that ran movies all night. Stephen sat with him for a while. It was a wonderful sight, the two of them together, but Keith was in so much pain that many times I had to leave the room just so he wouldn't see the tears. A few times the pain seemed so severe that I wondered if he'd last the night.

Worried, I telephoned his doctor. She immediately called the pharmacy and ordered a prescription for morphine patches.

When Keith was a little more comfortable, I offered him something to eat. He wanted cereal. "Okay, but I'll make a hamburger, too. A full stomach will help you to sleep better," I told him.

He tried to eat the hamburger first, just to make me happy, but in the end, I gave him the cereal. I was happy that at least he was eating something.

Stephen had gone up to bed, but I couldn't leave Keith yet. We sat watching television.

"Mom, are you mad at me?" he asked.

"Don't be silly, why would I be mad at you?"

"I'll be fine, Mom, really. I don't want you to worry."

"Of course you will . . . and I am not worried. Now get some rest."

I sat with Keith most of the night as he drifted in and out of sleep. Finally, just before dawn, he insisted that I go to bed. I was exhausted from staying up all night and from the emotional haze, so I agreed. After about an hour, I heard Keith, as he came to my bedroom door to check on me.

"Just making sure you're getting some rest," he said before heading back to the den.

NEVER SAY NEVER

Keith slept on and off throughout the morning. I only got a few hours of sleep, but it was enough. Mary came back later that day to pick Keith up and the two of them went to spend the night at her parents' house.

The following morning, Mary called.

"We need a van."

"For what?" I asked.

"Keith collapsed on the kitchen floor."

"Call an ambulance. Now! You need to call an ambulance."

"He doesn't want one. Call one anyway. We'll be right there."

Stephen insisted I stay home while he went over to see what was going on.

"You go get dressed," he told me. "I'll be back to get you in a little while."

I was almost ready when Stephen came back.

"The paramedics think it may have been an overdose of morphine. They're taking him to the hospital, but he's conscious."

The phone rang a few minutes later. Mary called from the hospital. She was hysterical. Keith had been intubated. It didn't look good. I had to get to the hospital right away.

I screamed at Stephen the whole way. "Hurry, Stephen, hurry. Go faster! We have to get there. Hurry."

"Calm down, Celeste. We don't know for sure what's happening. We'll be there soon. Just hang on."

We pulled into the parking lot, practically abandoning the car, and raced through the doors of the emergency room. The guards tried to stop us, but when we told them who we were they escorted us straight to the back where the doctors explained what was going on. Keith was unconscious, hooked up to monitors, and breathing with the help of a ventilator.

Mary was inconsolable and we held her tight, trying desperately to calm her, but by now we were all pretty upset. The doctor on call was waiting for Keith's oncologist to get back to him.

"I want to see my son," I demanded.

The nurse led me down a long hall to where Keith was. "Keith," I whispered into his ear. "There's no need to worry. Everything's going to be fine. I'm here now and I'm going to take care of you."

"Excuse me," a different nurse had poked her head in and asked to speak to me privately. She walked me back to the room where we had just met with the doctors. "Keith's oncologist called. He spoke to the ER doctor. They're in agreement that Keith has little chance of regaining consciousness. The recommendation is to take him off of life support," she explained.

"No. Absolutely not. Now leave me alone."

The nurse left the room and apparently went to find Stephen because seconds later

he came in and took me in his arms. "Celeste, it's time. You need to say good-bye, honey. This isn't what you want for him." Tears dribbled down his cheeks as he stepped back and looked deeply into my eyes. "You know I love you and I love Keith, too, but it's in God's hands now."

"Leave me alone. I need to think," was all I could say.

Stephen went to sit with Keith while I just sat there with my head in my hands. Mary came in and took a seat next to me.

"We need to do this," she said. "He's ready, but I can't do it alone. Please, help me. We need to let him go." She sobbed, dabbing at her face with a wad of tissues.

I looked at her, but didn't say a word. I couldn't.

Mary walked out and a woman in a navy suit came in.

"And what do you want? Better yet, just leave me alone and go away."

"I'm the hospital administrator and I need just a moment of your time. Please. We understand how difficult this time is and we want you to know that we'll do everything we can to help you. If you do decide to take your son off the ventilator, it's very possible that he'll continue to breathe on his own. There's no way to know for sure, but if he does we'll take each day as it comes and continue his care on our hospice floor."

NEVER SAY NEVER

When I didn't respond, she left. A few minutes later, a nurse came in and took a seat next to me.

"I know this isn't easy," she said. "Losing a child never is. It's the hardest thing a parent has to face. But the fact remains, Keith is going to die. There's no question about that. And he needs your help to do it."

"You're asking me to help my son die?" It was absurd. The woman was insane.

"I've seen this before," she said. "No matter how much pain or how long the struggle, a loved one won't leave until the family is ready."

I stared at her in disbelief.

"I'm asking you to give Keith permission to die."

I wiped the tears as they fell. It took every ounce of courage and it just about killed me, but I signed the paper right after Mary did. I knew Keith wouldn't have wanted her to carry the burden alone.

I went back to see Keith. This time I kissed him on the cheek, and then smiled softly at the memory of holding him for the first time.

"Did you know you've always been the best part of me? I wish there was a way for you to understand how much I love you. Listen to me, Keith. The fight is over, honey. I'm so proud of you. You won, baby. God's calling you home now. It's time to let go. There's nothing to worry about. I'll be okay. I promise."

The nurse came in and said it was time. She asked if I'd like to wait outside. I just couldn't watch. Mary went in and stayed with him. Her mother went in and stayed with her. After it was done, they asked if I'd like to see Keith again.

"Yes," I said and went back inside. I gave him another big kiss. "I love you now just as I have every single day from the minute you were born. From now until eternity, Keith, you'll always be with me and I'll always love you."

Back in the hallway, crushing pain gave way to racking sobs. It came out in one huge torrent, as Stephen held me in his arms and gently stroked my hair.

The administrator came over and touched my shoulder. "Keith's gone," she said. "He's at peace."

It was eerily silent when I went in to see my son for the last time. Tubes and wires had all been disconnected, the ventilator and monitors all turned off. I gently traced the lines of his face, the arch of his brow, memorizing his every feature as I sniffed back tears. "You're my angel and we'll always be together," I whispered, my voice cracking.

Keith's oncologist had warned us to be prepared for the end. But how do you do that? How do you give up hope and accept that your child is going to die?

Stephen held me close as we walked through the maze of corridors and out into the afternoon sun. The weatherman had said it was going to be a beautiful day. I put my sunglasses on. He couldn't have been more wrong.

CHAPTER THIRTY-FIVE

I always wanted to be normal, but I'm not. It wasn't normal to be abused and it wasn't normal to marry a drunk, and it's definitely not normal for a parent to bury a child.

I never experienced the love of a mother, but I do understand what it means now. It's when you want to make everything right for your child but you're helpless to do a thing. It's what keeps you there anyway, patiently waiting for the chance. I'm headstrong, determined, and very willing to speak out. I'm not easily intimidated, nor do I ever give up. And those, it turned out, were precisely the characteristics that Keith relied upon. It's who I became in spite of what I suffered.

I no longer have the need to overcome my childhood because that battle's been won. And while beginnings are scary and endings are sad, it's the middle where you find out exactly who you are and what you're made of.

As time went on, I accepted Keith's death by focusing on his life. He had the normal life that I always wanted. He had a mother who made sure he'd want for nothing, a loving home with a father and grandparents who doted on him. And when he was grown, he found the love of his life and married her.

Some days I can hear Keith laughing. "Mom you're relentless," his words echo in my ears. Other days, all I can hear is the sound of my own heart breaking.

CELESTE ROTH

Though I've suffered many losses, not one prepared me for losing my son. Grieving was a process that I knew couldn't be rushed. The only consolation was that I was there for my son when he needed me most. Keith had finally opened his heart and allowed me to be a mother to him.

IN MEMORY OF

Keith Michael Shank
August 10, 1979 - June 19, 2006

ABOUT THE AUTHOR

Celeste Roth lives in New York with her husband, Stephen, and their two dogs, Ozzy and Boo Boo.

CPSIA information can be obtained at www.ICGtesting.com
Printed in the USA
BVOW01s0340300914

368777BV00001B/47/P